THE BILL ON LONDON

The Bill on London

or, the Finance of Trade
by Bills of Exchange

Published for
GILLETT BROTHERS DISCOUNT COMPANY LTD
65 Cornhill, London EC3V 3PP
by Methuen & Co Ltd

Published in 1952 by Chapman & Hall Ltd
11 New Fetter Lane, London EC4
for Gillett Brothers Discount Company Ltd
65 Cornhill, London EC3V 3PP
Second revised edition 1959
Third revised edition 1964

Fourth revised edition 1976
published by Methuen & Co Ltd
11 New Fetter Lane, London EC4

© Gillett Brothers Discount Company Ltd

ISBN 416 85670 5

Design & typography Ron Costley/Shenval
Printed in England by
Shenval Press, London and Harlow

Contents

Foreword   *page* 11
Dramatis personæ   12
What is a bill?   15

PART ONE   THE STORY OF THE BILL
   I   History of the bill of exchange   19
  II   The functions of the bill   20
 III   'Term' and 'sight' bills   21
 IV   Credits   22
  V   The quality of a bill   22
        A The names on the bill
        B The nature of the transaction underlying the bill
 VI   Your name on a bill   26
 VII   The discounting of a bill   26
VIII   The cost of bill finance   27

PART TWO   THE BILL IN ACTION
   I   The bill of exchange and the exporter   31
        Method 1 The irrevocable documentary letter of credit
        Method 2 London acceptance credit
        Method 3 The negotiated bill
        Method 4 The foreign domicile bill
  II   The bill of exchange and the importer   39
        Method A The irrevocable documentary letter of credit
        Method B London acceptance credit
        Method C The negotiated (trade) bill
        Note on bank endorsed bills
 III   The bill of exchange and the manufacturer   46
 IV   Trade bills   49
  V   The bill of exchange and the international trader   51

VI   Remitted bills   53
      The bill on London and the foreign banker
      A Financing exports
      B Financing imports
VII   A parcel of bills   57
VIII   The bill of exchange and the investor   59
IX   Conclusion   60

PART THREE PROCEDURE

I   The bill of exchange and the exporter   63
     1   Irrevocable documentary letter of credit issued by a bank or accepting house in favour of the Exporting Company.
     2   Revolving acceptance credit covering exports from the U.K. to Atlantis opened in favour of the Exporting Company by William Caxton & Co—unsecured.
     3   Revolving acceptance credit covering exports from the U.K. to Atlantis opened in favour of the Exporting Company by William Caxton & Co—secured.
II   The bill of exchange and the importer   74
     4   Irrevocable documentary letter of credit in favour of an overseas exporter opened by a bank or accepting house.
     5   Revolving acceptance credit covering shipments of wool to the U.K. opened in favour of the Importing Company by William Caxton & Co—unsecured.
     6   Revolving acceptance credit covering shipments of wool to the U.K. opened in favour of the Importing Company by William Caxton & Co—secured.
III   The bill of exchange and the manufacturer   86
     7   Revolving acceptance credit covering purchases of cocoa and other materials, opened in favour of the Manufacturing Company by William Caxton & Co—unsecured.
IV   The bill of exchange and the investor   91

PART FOUR   GLOSSARY AND INDEX

Glossary and index   95

Illustrations

Figure

1   The face of a bill   *page* 14
2   An export bill (irrevocable documentary letter of credit)   32
3   An export bill (London acceptance credit)   34
4   An export bill (foreign domicile)   38
5   An import bill (irrevocable documentary letter of credit)   40
6   An import bill (London acceptance credit)   42
7   An import bill (negotiated (trade) bill)   44
8   A manufacturer's bill   48
9   A trade bill   50
10 An international trader's bill (London acceptance credit)   52
11 A continental importer's bill   56
2a An export bill (irrevocable documentary letter of credit) – accepted and endorsed   64
3a An export bill (London acceptance credit) – accepted and endorsed   71
5a An import bill (irrevocable documentary letter of credit) – accepted and endorsed   76
6a An import bill (London acceptance credit) – accepted and endorsed   81
8a A manufacturer's bill – accepted and endorsed   88

All these bills, with acceptance and endorsement, will be found (with the exception of No. 4) in the pocket at the end of the book.

ACKNOWLEDGMENTS

Our most grateful thanks are due to a number of friends in the City who have freely given us the benefit of their knowledge and experience, spending many hours on the correction and improvement of our original drafts.

We acknowledge with thanks the courtesy of The New Era Publishing Co in allowing us to make use of Thomson's *Dictionary of Banking* in the compilation of the Glossary. Any help we needed with works of reference was provided by the librarian of the Institute of Bankers, to whom we return thanks.

We have welcomed the comments of our readers and have incorporated a number of their suggestions for additions and improvements in this revised edition.

The quotation on page 61 is from Rudyard Kipling's 'In the Neolithic Age' from *Barrack Room Ballads* and is printed by kind permission of the late Mrs George Bambridge, the owner of the copyright, and of Messrs Methuen & Co Ltd.

'*The City of London can still claim to be
the most highly organised international market
for money in the world.
Its freedom and elasticity are without parallel.
Its accepting houses and discount houses
provide unequalled facilities
for the financing of national
and international commerce.*'

MACMILLAN REPORT, 1930

Foreword

'To Merchants, Traders, Importers, Exporters and Manufacturers, these notes on "The Bill on London" are offered in the hope that the traditional method of finance by Bills may become better known, more easily understood and more widely used.

The City of London is the financial centre of the world, and the London Money Market has long been the Market, beyond all others, to which merchants from Britain and many other countries come for the finance of trade.

To us, as a Discount House, Bills are our stock-in-trade. The more good Bills there are, the better for the Discount Market, and the better for us, who get our share.

We shall welcome any enquiries about Bill Finance, and shall be glad to explain or to enlarge upon any points which are not clear. We believe that it is to the advantage of any business which draws Bills of Exchange to be in direct touch with a Discount House, which has much to offer in experience and knowledge of the London Money Market, where Bills are bought and sold.'

Ronald Gillett, chairman from 1946 until his death in 1965, wrote those words as the Foreword to the first edition. They remain as true today as when they were written twenty-five years ago.

The intervening period has seen the development of new money markets and financial centres overseas in almost all cases successfully modelled on London practice and the 'Bill on London'.

We hope that the fourth edition of our book will continue to help in some measure towards a better understanding of the traditional usage of bills in domestic and international markets throughout the world.

June 1976

David Whitton   *Chairman*

GILLETT BROTHERS DISCOUNT COMPANY LTD
65 CORNHILL, LONDON EC3V 3PP

DRAMATIS PERSONÆ

THE LOMBARD BANK A London clearing bank

THE CLEARING BANK Another London clearing bank

WILLIAM CAXTON & CO. A London accepting house

GILLETT BROTHERS DISCOUNT COMPANY LTD. A London discount
house

THE BANK OF ATLANTIS An overseas bank with a branch office in
London

THE BANK OF EUROPA A foreign bank with no branch office in London

THE BANK OF RURITANIA Another foreign bank with no branch office in
London

THE BANK OF ASIA An Eastern Exchange bank with a London Office

THE EXPORTING CO. A British exporter

THE IMPORTING CO. A British importer

THE WOOLBUYING CO. A firm through whom the Importing Co buys
wool

THE MANUFACTURING CO. A British manufacturer

THE TRADER A British trader in goods for sale to industry in the UK

THE INDUSTRIAL CO. A British industrial company which buys some of its
raw materials from the trader

THE INTERNATIONAL TRADER A British trader in commodities in various
parts of the World

THE CONTINENTAL IMPORTER A foreign importer, customer of the Bank
of Europa

THE TEA ESTATE An exporter of tea from Islandia to the UK

THE LONDON BLENDER A British importer of tea from Islandia

THE OVERSEAS IMPORTER A trader in another country who imports
goods from the UK

NOTE

With three exceptions all names used throughout the book are imaginary. Any resemblance to the name of any existing firm or institution is a coincidence. The exceptions are the Bank of England, the Export Credits Guarantee Department of the Department of Trade and Industry, and our own name Gillett Brothers.

Gillett Brothers Discount Co Ltd, a member of the London Discount Market Association, was founded in 1867. One of the principal activities of such a firm is buying and selling bills of exchange, as described in this book. As a discount house Gilletts also deal in day-to-day money, principally with London bankers, and in British government Treasury bills and short-dated bonds, Local authority bills and bonds, sterling certificates of deposit, dollar certificates of deposit and bills of exchange in currencies other than sterling.

We have chosen the name William Caxton & Co for our accepting house.

William Caxton (1422–91), a member of the London Mercers' Company or Guild, traded for thirty years in the Low Countries. There he became interested in printing, procured equipment and workmen, and brought them to London. He founded his Press at Westminster in 1476 and introduced the art and craft of printing to this country. He and men like him were forerunners of those who in the nineteenth century founded in London the great accepting houses for the finance of international trade. It is with due respect to the memory of a great Englishman that we use his name.

An accepting house is a firm of bankers specialising in the arrangement of short-term finance by granting acceptance credits (see p. 22). Under these credits bills of exchange are drawn on and 'accepted' by the accepting house, and are then negotiable instruments which may be discounted (i.e. sold at a discount for cash) with a London discount house. The accepting house, by accepting, make themselves responsible for payment of the bill at maturity, and it is primarily on the strength of their name that the discount house provides the cash. For thus lending their name the accepting house will charge a commission.

Accepting houses may also take deposits, make loans, deal in foreign exchange, act as principals in the arrangement of capital issues, and engage in many other banking activities.

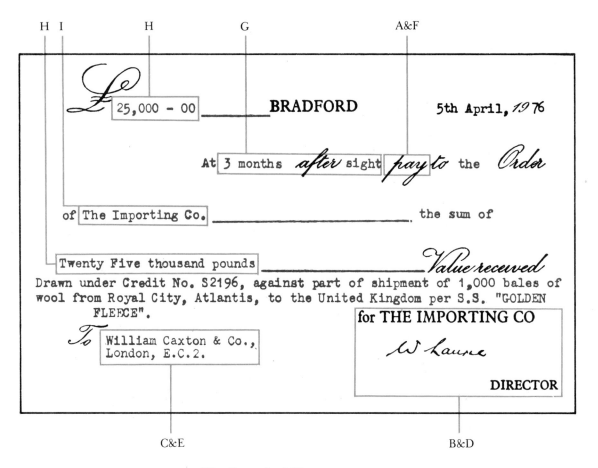

FIGURE I The face of a bill

A An unconditional order in writing
B addressed by one person (*The drawer*)
C to another (*The drawee*)
D signed by the person giving it (*The drawer*)
E requiring the person to whom it is addressed
(*The drawee, who when he signs becomes The acceptor*)
F to pay
G on demand, or at a fixed or determinable future time
H a sum certain in money
I to, or to the order of, a specified person, or to bearer (*The payee*)

WHAT IS A BILL?

A bill of exchange is defined by the Bills of Exchange Act, 1882:

A BILL OF EXCHANGE IS
an unconditional order in writing
addressed by one person to another
signed by the person giving it
requiring the person to whom it is addressed
to pay
on demand or at a fixed or determinable future time
a sum certain in money
to or to the order of a specified person
or to bearer 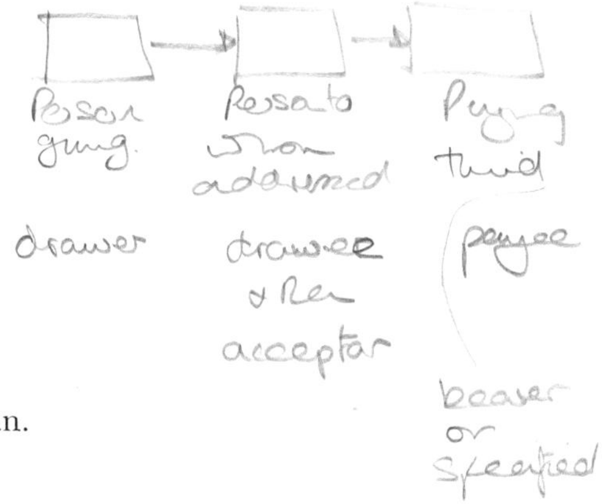
Fig. 1 (on the opposite page) shows what these phrases mean.

[Handwritten annotations to the right: "Person giving" — "drawer"; "Person to whom addressed" — "drawee & acc / acceptor"; "Paying third" — "payee"; "bearer or specified"]

A BILL ON LONDON IS
a bill of exchange
addressed to a drawee in the United Kingdom
and payable in London

THE PARTIES TO A BILL
The parties to a bill of exchange are the drawer, the acceptor, the payee and the endorser(s).

The drawer is the person who draws the bill. The acceptor is the person to whom the bill is addressed and who shows his assent by signing his name across the bill indicating that he will pay the bill at maturity. The payee is the person to whom or to whose order the bill is drawn payable. An endorser is a payee or any other person who signs his name on the bill. The rights and responsibilities attached to these, the parties to the bill, are severally defined in the glossary at the end of the book.

Part one
The story of the bill

'You have devised and sustained
a most marvellous system of credit.'

DISRAELI to the House of Commons (1866)

Blah — Blah Blah
Blah
auth
nty
agne caness ——▶ wd - anao

I HISTORY OF THE BILL OF EXCHANGE

The bill is one of the oldest instruments of credit in the world, and we can trace its origins far back in classical history. Thus in the fourth century BC the Greeks made use of bills. That credit standing and the value of a good name were already well understood is instanced by a story by Herodotus. Writing three generations after the failure of one Glaucus to honour a bill in defiance of oracular advice from Delphi, Herodotus describes him, his descendants, and even any of his house, as being 'utterly extirpated from Sparta'.

Later Cicero and others show in their writings that the Romans drew bills on their agents in other countries, but if the Romans introduced the bill into England we have no record of it. Not until the Norman conquest, when jews first came to this country, are bills of exchange recorded in common use, and they are officially mentioned first in a statute of 1379 under Richard II. Meanwhile, on the continent, bills had survived the dark ages. They are known to have been in common use in Florence, Siena, Hamburg and Venice in the twelfth and thirteenth centuries, and subject to control by French and Venetian statute law.

The next important date is 1697 when inland bills were made legal in England. From then on the use of bills in this country increased considerably. At least until the middle of the nineteenth century they were widely used in connection with domestic trade, and in some centres formed part of the currency of the district, since bills bearing the names of local firms and individuals of high standing changed from hand to hand in settlement of debts. Not only were bills the principal means of payment for all except very small sums, but discounting bills with a bank was the usual method of obtaining bank accommodation. At that time the banking system of the country was made up of a great number of small private banks. According to their requirements these banks bought or sold bills through the London discount market, which thus provided a means of transmitting the surplus money in the hands of banks in the agricultural areas to the banks in the developing industrial areas.

By the second half of the nineteenth century, bills had become such an important method of finance and so widely used that, to facilitate their use, successive statutory rules were codified in the Bills of Exchange Act, 1882. By this act bill transactions are governed today.

The development of joint stock banking, with its system of cash transfers between branches, and the growing custom of granting overdraft facilities, led to a reduction in the use of bills for domestic finance during the nineteenth century. On the other hand the establishment in London of branches of foreign banks, and the rise of the London accepting houses, resulted in the great development of the international bill on London.

With Britain on the gold standard, bills accepted by first class London houses were the same as gold, as they could always be discounted in the London discount market, the proceeds converted into gold if the state of the exchanges justified it, and the gold taken out of the country to any part of the world. This gave the £ bill on London the supreme position which it held during the years over the turn of the century, as the predominant instrument for the finance of international trade.

Since 1914, there have been vast disturbances of international trade and finance, and the use of bills has at times been greatly reduced, but as trade revives the Bill on London once more comes into its own. A financial instrument which has stood the test of centuries must be of interest to every business man.

II THE FUNCTIONS OF THE BILL

The primary function of the bill is to enable the seller or exporter of goods to obtain cash as soon as possible after the despatch of the goods, and yet enable the buyer or importer to defer payment until the goods reach him, or later.

The seller and the buyer are often separated from each other by great distances. In international trade they may have to contend also with fluctuating exchange rates, and other technical problems not easy to assess. For buyer and seller, whether they are in different countries or in the same country, a bank or accepting house acts as an intermediary on whom both can rely; lending an undoubted name; taking off their shoulders the burden of financing the goods in transit from one to the other; and helping to ensure that each observes towards the other the agreed financial conditions of their business deals. The bill is the instrument through which a bank or accepting house can thus act.

A further function of the bill is to provide essential short term finance for trade and industry. In this context the bill is frequently ancillary to the bank advance but should not altogether take its place. Bill finance is temporary finance, to be used for specific transactions or for seasonal or other short-term requirements, which would not justify raising more permanent capital.

Some of the ways in which the bill fulfils these functions are set out in the following pages. The manner in which the various methods described can in practice be used may, in those countries including the United Kingdom which have Exchange Control, depend on the rules in force at the time.

III 'TERM' & 'SIGHT' BILLS

Up to this point, we have for the most part had in mind bills drawn in such a way as to be payable after a period of time, such as ninety days. Bills may be drawn for any period, the most usual being ninety days, or three months, but many are drawn for anything from thirty days to six months. These 'term' bills are negotiable instruments which may be bought and sold on the London discount market.

Mention must also be made, however, of 'sight' bills, i.e. bills drawn payable at sight, or on demand. As sight bills are paid immediately they are presented to the person on whom they are drawn, the question of discounting them does not arise. For this reason, little further mention of them will be found in this book, but it may be said that the underlying principles and procedure for a bill drawn at sight are very similar to those described as applicable to a 'term' bill.

It should be remembered, too, that a very substantial part of international trade is financed by means of sight bills, particularly at a time of sellers' markets. When markets are favouring buyers the seller may find that he has to accord longer credit terms to the buyer, and this will lead to the drawing of 'term' bills, or, as they are sometimes known in international trade, 'usance' bills.

IV CREDITS

Frequent mention is made of 'credits', and it may be useful to define them here. A credit, for our purposes, means any arrangement with bankers by which they are to pay or accept bills of exchange on behalf of a customer.

When the bills are presented to the banks or accepting houses on whom they are drawn, the drawees 'accept' them by signing across the bill a promise to pay at the end of the period. Accepted bills are often called 'acceptances'.

OPENING A CREDIT

A prospective borrower may go to his own bank and discuss the possibility of opening a credit.

Alternatively he may decide that the business he has in mind would be more suitable for an accepting house, in which case he may go to one with which he has direct connections and seek to arrange a credit. If, on the other hand, he is already in touch with a discount house he may consult with them as to the best method and the best approach.

The accepting house will decide, on the basis of information provided by the prospective borrower, whether or not they are prepared, in principle, to grant a credit. If they are prepared to grant a credit, the detailed terms will be the subject of negotiation. If agreement is reached, formal expression is given to it by the issue by the accepting house, to the borrower, of a facility letter or a letter of credit.

A number of examples of typical facility letters and letters of credit are given in part three (Procedure).

V THE QUALITY OF A BILL

There are many classes of bill which may be drawn and many types of credit providing for the drawing of bills which may be arranged. In the following pages will be found notes addressed to each of the main potential users of bills outlining the principal ways in which the bill may be used to suit them best. There are, however, some points of general interest to all who are considering bill finance. These concern what may be called the *quality of a bill*.

The quality of a bill will be judged from two things, first the standing (good name and capital resources) of the drawer and the acceptor, and second the nature of the transaction against which the bill is drawn.

A – THE NAMES ON THE BILL

Fine bank bills

Fine bank bills are bills drawn on, and accepted by, London banks and accepting houses of undoubted standing. Such bills command the finest rates of discount.

Notice will also be taken of the name of the drawer, even though it is on the name of the acceptor that the bill is judged.

Foreign bank bills

Foreign bank bills are bills drawn on and accepted by the London branches of overseas banks, i.e. banks whose head offices are located abroad. Some of these banks enjoy the highest standing in the London market and fine rates are quoted for their acceptances.

Trade bills

Trade bills are bills drawn by one trader on another. A fuller note on these will be found on p 49. Suffice it here to say that the rates quoted for trade bills are customarily higher than those quoted for fine bank or foreign bank bills and that the total amount of trade bills that can be marketed on the strength of the name of any one drawer or acceptor is limited.

'Foreign domicile' bills

These are bills drawn on and accepted by banks, companies or individuals abroad. No matter how good the names of the acceptor and the drawer may be such bills are not saleable in the London discount market. The holder of a foreign domicile bill may get an advance against it from his bankers if he hands it to them for collection, but he cannot rely on being able to sell it to a discount house, since a foreign domicile bill would not be good security for a discount house to place against its loans from the banks. A bill accepted by a foreign bank, let us say by the Bank of Ruritania, which has no London Office, is a foreign domicile bill, and its character is not altered even if the Bank of Ruritania inscribes on the face of the bill 'payable at The Lombard

Bank, London . . .'; but such a bill may possibly be placed in the London discount market if it is endorsed by a London bank, which thus guarantees to the holder that he will receive payment in London. (See: 'Note on bank endorsed bills', p 46.)

It is most important to exporters that they should be aware of the limitations of foreign domicile bills. The exporter to Ruritania, for example, should not be satisfied, unless he has no option, with a credit opened in his favour and available by drafts on the Bank of Ruritania abroad. He should insist that the credit be opened in London with a London bank or accepting house on whom he can draw. He will then have a bill which he can discount in the London discount market, and thus obtain immediate £ funds.

See also: 'The Bill of exchange and the exporter', *Method four,* p 36.

B—THE NATURE OF THE TRANSACTION UNDERLYING THE BILL

The documentary bill

When a bill is drawn to cover an actual movement of goods from the seller to the buyer, and the relative documents (bill of lading, insurance policy etc.) are attached to the bill when it is drawn, the bill is known as a documentary bill.

The buyer of the goods may ask the seller to draw a term bill on him direct (trade bill), or he may open a credit in favour of the seller with a London bank or accepting house, on whom the seller will draw his bill (fine bank bill). In either case the bill both before and after it is accepted is negotiable. The seller of the goods can sell it for immediate cash to his local bankers or, after it is accepted, to a London discount house. The seller is thus paid for his goods when they are despatched. The buyer for his part does not have to pay until the bill, having been duly accepted, matures, and this will usually be after the goods have reached their destination and have been re-sold.

If the bill is drawn on the buyer himself he must meet it at maturity, while, if the bill is drawn on a London banker under a credit opened on behalf of the buyer, he must put the banker in funds by the maturity date on which the banker has to pay the bill. During the lifetime of the bill the goods are on the move across the seas, or have reached warehouse, or are otherwise in course of resale or use, and the period of the perfect bill is just enough to span the interval between shipment by the exporter and receipt of cash from the resale by the importer. The buyer may have contracted beforehand to sell the goods to a customer of his own, the proceeds of the sale providing the cash to meet the bill. In such a case the bill is aptly described as 'self-liquidating', but bills are in practice regarded as self-liquidating when it is in the normal course of the buyer's business to sell the underlying goods.

Here it is appropriate to point out to buyers of goods an important advantage in having bills drawn on and accepted by their bankers or an accepting house, instead of themselves. If there has been a delay in the arrival of the goods, or if for any other unforeseen reason the buyer is not in funds when a bill which he has accepted falls due for payment, he must nevertheless pay the bill, and it might be highly inconvenient, or in difficult times even impossible, for him to do so. The holder of the bill will have the right of immediate action against him. If, however, he has arranged for a bank or accepting house to accept the bill for him, the bill will certainly be paid to the holder at its maturity.

When a bill is drawn to finance a movement or shipment of goods the drawer should put on the face of the bill a few words describing the nature of the transaction. For example, 'exports of machine tools to South Africa per S.S. *Fortress*', or 'imports of *x* bales of wool from Australia per S.S. *Golden Fleece*'. The insertion of such phrases is commonly called 'clausing'. Clausing makes clear the nature of the transaction which is being financed. The banks, who buy bills from the discount houses, like to see evidence of the underlying transaction, and the clausing answers in advance questions which might otherwise be asked. It is a wise precaution, when dealing with instruments of credit, to make any questioning of the underlying transaction unnecessary.

It remains true, however, that although any evidence of the nature of the underlying transaction will be studied by any one who is asked to discount a bill, or to accept it as security for a loan, the respect enjoyed by a bill of exchange depends above all on the standing and credit of the acceptor and the drawer.

The finance bill

There is much discussion of the meaning of the term 'finance bill', and no exact definition can be given without fear of contradiction. Indeed it often happens that one expert inspecting a bill will give his opinion that it is a finance bill, while another, equally well qualified to judge, will argue that it is not.

In a general way it may be said that nowadays bills drawn to finance the holding or processing of stocks of raw materials, or to enable the drawer to give credit to his customer by hire purchase or by simple credit terms, are frequently but not invariably described as finance bills.

City institutions which deal in bills do not always look on finance bills as being quite such attractive investments as bills covering the movement of goods, and the amount of finance paper that can be discounted in the market or at the Bank of England may be limited. None the less, many of the finest names to be found on bills in the market have at times been on finance bills, drawn to supply working capital for a limited period until it could be favourably obtained by a share or debenture issue. Many first class bills have been drawn not 'for value received', but merely as a convenient means of taking a loan.

Since a finance bill is not linked to a specific underlying transaction or movement of goods its quality is even more dependent on the names of the drawer and the acceptor. The less the evidence of an actual transaction underlying a bill, the stronger these names must be.

VI   YOUR NAME ON A BILL

Two good names on a bill give quality to the bill. They also lend lustre to each other. Nothing adds so much to the standing of even the greatest firms, as to be seen to enjoy the confidence in each other which is implied by the association of their two names on a bill.

VII THE DISCOUNTING OF A BILL

To avoid confusion we shall use the term 'discounting' a bill to mean, for the owner of the bill, selling it, once it is duly accepted, to a bank or discount house in London. For the bank or discount house it will mean buying the bill.

Bills change hands before they are accepted, but these deals are usually described as simply buying or selling bills, or 'negotiating' them. A bill is not ready to be discounted in London until it is accepted.

A bill is the property of the drawer until he sells or discounts it; once sold, it belongs to the buyer. And, the acceptor having played his part by signing across the bill his promise to pay, it is to the drawer or owner of the bill, or to his order, that the proceeds of discounting will be paid. The drawer or owner therefore has the right to decide with whom the bill shall be discounted, although practice varies.

From common experience it may be said that banks or accepting houses will usually tell the drawer or owner of a bill that he is free to discount it when, and with whom he wishes. They will also tell the drawer or owner that they are quite willing to act on his instructions to hand the bill for discount to a discount house named by him, or, if he prefers, to a discount house of their own choice. Where a merchant abroad sells a bill to local bankers, clearly it will be their London agents who will decide which discount house to use.

NOTE: For the detailed procedure of discounting a bill and for a discount statement issued by Gillett Brothers Discount Company Ltd for a bill discounted with them, see Part III (Procedure).

VIII   THE COST OF BILL FINANCE

The cost to a borrower of raising money by means of an acceptance credit varies according to the business.

To a merchant or manufacturer financing purchases of raw materials, the cost will be made up of the accepting commission charged by the bank or accepting house, plus the rate of discount at which the bills are sold to the discount house. The accepting commission is a matter for negotiation with the banker and the rate of discount for a bank bill varies with the present and prospective rates for money. See note on discount rates page 62.

If the borrower is an importer, however, who arranges for a seller abroad to draw on a London bank or accepting house, the importer has to pay the accepting commission, but the cost of selling a bill locally and/or discounting it in London, will usually fall on the seller, who may or may not include part or all of the cost in his invoice. It is possible, and it is frequently done, to arrange in the credit for these costs to be borne by the buyer, in which case either the seller will receive on presenting his bill the face value thereof plus the cost of local bill stamps, if any, or, if he sells or discounts the bill himself, the costs incurred will be reimbursed to him. The charge made by the discounter for discounting a bill is simply a rate of discount per annum for providing the money for the lifetime of the bill.

Indications of the current rates at which the discount market will buy bills are given every day in the financial columns of *The Times*. They appear as part of a table of money and bill rates under the heading 'MONEY MARKET RATES'. Similar information is given daily in *The Financial Times*.

NOTE: Any discount rate quoted is a rate per cent *per annum*. Thus a discount rate of 8·5% for 3 months means 8·5% per annum charged for 3 months, which is equivalent to an actual charge of 2·125%.

Part two
The bill in action

'Then said the Interpreter,
          "Come in: I will show thee
that which will be profitable to thee".'

JOHN BUNYAN

1 THE BILL OF EXCHANGE AND THE EXPORTER

TO THE EXPORTING COMPANY

You are an exporter of finished goods from the UK to Atlantis and your overseas importer requires credit. This means that you will have to finance the shipment while it is in transit, and possibly for some weeks after its arrival in the country to which you have sent it. There are a number of ways in which the bill of exchange may help you.

METHOD ONE : *The irrevocable documentary letter of credit*
By far the best procedure is for you to ask your customer to open in your favour an irrevocable documentary letter of credit with a London bank. Under this method he requests his own bank in Atlantis, the Bank of Atlantis, to open a credit in your favour. As the Bank of Atlantis have a London office which enjoys a very high standing in the market they will request this office to issue to you an irrevocable letter of credit. In this letter of credit the London office of the Bank of Atlantis undertake to accept a bill drawn on them by you, against surrender to them of the shipping documents relating to the goods. A specimen of the letter of credit opened in your favour by the Bank of Atlantis will be found on p. 63.

When your bill drawn under this credit has been accepted by the Bank of Atlantis, London, you can at once offer it to a discount house who will discount it for you (i.e. buy it from you at a discount) at an agreed rate (see 'foreign bank bills', p. 23).

Whether you bear the cost of discounting the bill, or whether you include this charge separately in your invoice or in the price of your goods, will depend on your contract with the buyer. He himself will normally be responsible for the accepting commission, and when the bill matures he has to put the Bank of Atlantis in funds to meet the bill.

An example of a bill drawn under this method appears on the next page at fig 2.

The procedure for financing exports to a foreign customer whose bank, the Bank of Europa, has not an office in London is very similar. The differ-

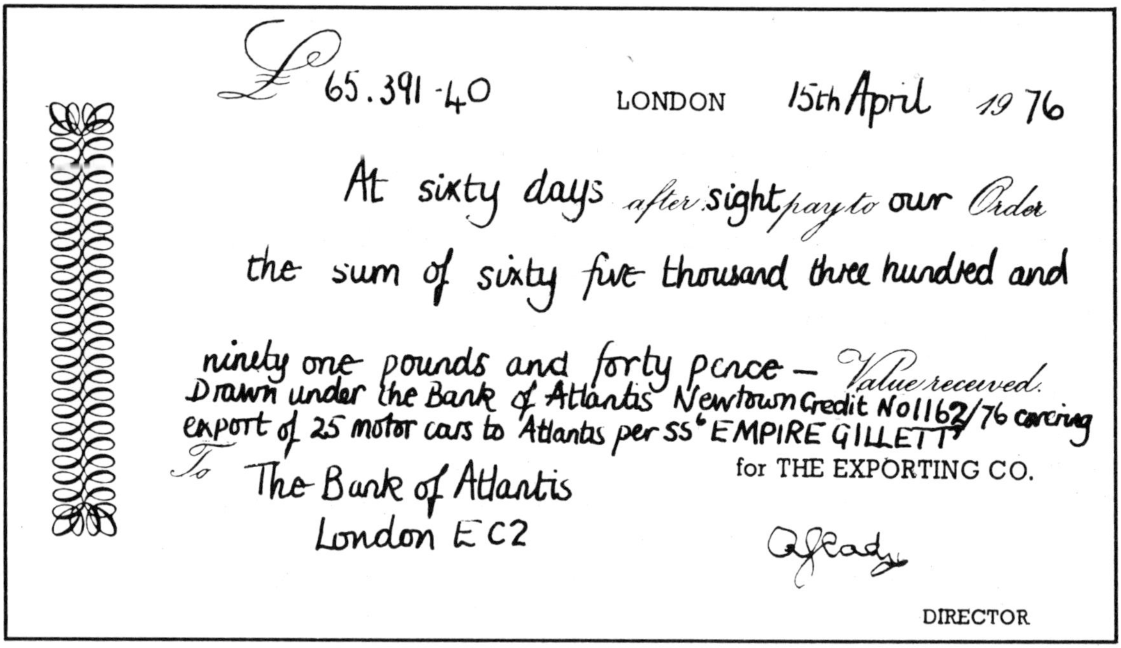

£ 65.391-40　　　　LONDON　　15th April　19 76

At sixty days *after sight pay to* our *Order*

the sum of sixty five thousand three hundred and

ninety one pounds and forty pence — *Value received.*
Drawn under the Bank of Atlantis Newtown Credit No 1162/76 covering
export of 25 motor cars to Atlantis per SS "EMPIRE GILLETT" 76

To The Bank of Atlantis
　　　London EC2

for THE EXPORTING CO.

O'Grady

DIRECTOR

FIGURE 2
An export bill drawn by The Exporting Co, London, on the Bank of Atlantis under an
irrevocable documentary credit, as described on page 31.

The same bill, accepted by the Bank of Atlantis and endorsed by The Exporting Co, will be found at
fig 2a in part three (Procedure) on p 64, and again in the parcel of bills at the end of the book.

ence is that the Bank of Europa ask their London correspondents, the Lombard Bank, to advise you that they, the Bank of Europa, have opened an irrevocable credit in your favour, available by drawing bills on the Lombard Bank. This means that you rely on the strength of the Bank of Europa, but the Lombard Bank has given you no undertaking to accept your bill when you present it. However the Bank of Europa will, if you so stipulate in your contract, ask the Lombard Bank to confirm the credit to you, so binding themselves to accept your bill. In this case it is a confirmed irrevocable credit. See also p. 67.

METHOD TWO: *London acceptance credit*

Alternatively, you may yourself be able to obtain an acceptance credit from a London accepting house, or in some instances from another bank.

A – THE CREDIT

As yours is a company of good standing, and doing a valuable export trade, you will find there are a number of accepting houses which would be glad to help you with the finance. Let us suppose that you decide, whether for reasons of your own or on the advice of the discount house whom you have consulted, to discuss the business with Messrs William Caxton & Co, a well-known London accepting house.

You tell William Caxton that your annual exports total about £2,000,000, spread evenly over the year, so that you will have to find about £500,000 every three months. On this basis they agree to grant you an acceptance facility of say 80%, or £400,000, outstanding at any one time, so that if you have free capital of your own of about £100,000 you will with their assistance be able to find the whole amount. In other words, William Caxton agree to accept bills up to a running maximum of £400,000 drawn on them by you, at three months sight. Such a credit may be granted 'until further notice' or, by arrangement, for a fixed period such as one year, during which any bills that mature and are paid off may be replaced by other bills, when it is known as a revolving credit.

When your bills have been accepted by William Caxton you discount them with a discount house and receive your money. At the end of the three

£ 36 000 -00   LONDON   19th March 1976

At 90 days   after sight pay to the Order
of The Exporting Company —————

The sum of thirty six thousand pounds Value received.
Drawn under Credit No S3219 against shipment of
Agricultural Tractors to Atlantis per SS "Argonaut"

To   William Caxton & Co.,
     London, E.C.2.

for THE EXPORTING CO.

DIRECTOR

FIGURE 3
An export bill drawn by The Exporting Co, London, on William Caxton & Co under a
London acceptance credit as described on page 33.

The same bill, accepted by William Caxton & Co and endorsed by The Exporting Co, will be found at
fig 3a in part three (Procedure) on p 71, and again in the parcel of bills at the end of the book.

months, having met the first £400,000 of bills, you will probably have to produce to William Caxton evidence that a further £500,000 of export business is outstanding, against which you will be entitled to draw and discount a further £400,000 of bills.

B – SECURITY

The accepting house may require security, such as hypothecation to them of the relative shipping documents, but in some cases, and for borrowers of high standing, they are prepared to grant a 'clean' or 'unsecured' credit, on the understanding that they are furnished with evidence of the shipments or transactions against which the bill is drawn.

Where security is required this is a matter for negotiation between the accepting house and the borrower. In some cases the accepting house would wish to keep under their control the bills of lading or other documents of title covering your exports. These they would send to their own agent in the country to which your goods are consigned, for release to the importer against payment, or by other agreed arrangement.

It may be that you are accustomed to drawing trade bills (see p 49) on your overseas customers. If so, the accepting house may grant you the credit facility for which you are asking, against the collection of these bills, duly hypothecated, (i.e. made over) to them by way of security. All these and other essential details you will negotiate with the accepting house at the time of opening the credit.

An example of a bill drawn under method two appears opposite at fig 3.

Specimen facility letters issued to you an exporter, by William Caxton & Co, a London accepting house:

(i) granting unsecured facilities will be found on page 68, and

(ii) granting secured facilities, on page 69.

While these are the principal London bill methods in general use, you will find great flexibility in the approach of the accepting house to your particular problems. Provided that the parties to the transaction are of good standing, and the business is genuine export business, the finance will be forthcoming in the manner and on the terms appropriate to the case.

As you will know, exporters frequently insure their overseas business against the risk of non-payment, etc, with the Export Credits Guarantee Department of the Department of Trade and Industry. This gives an added sense of security to all parties to the credit, though no mention of this precaution will normally appear on the bills themselves, which are dealt in on their own merits.

METHOD THREE : *The negotiated bill negotiated under credit or authority to negotiate*

Exports to countries whose banks have branches in London, such as Atlantis, may be financed by means of bills to be negotiated under a credit.

The importer overseas, instead of opening an acceptance credit, or a credit providing for sight bills in London in your favour, arranges for the London office of the Bank of Atlantis to issue to you a credit, in which the bank undertakes to 'negotiate' bills drawn by you *on the importer.* You draw your bills on the importer and present them, with documents attached, to the Bank of Atlantis, London, which buys them from you for cash, and sends them out to the Bank of Atlantis, Atlantis. There the Bank of Atlantis hand the documents to your importer customer, the drawee, against payment, or at their discretion against acceptance if the bill is drawn at usance (i.e. for a period).

This method is traditional for many British exports to countries whose banks have branches in London, or London correspondents willing to act for them in this way; but these negotiated bills, having foreign domicile, are as we have already shown on page 23, not readily saleable on the London discount market.

METHOD FOUR : *The foreign domicile bill*

Your customer overseas asks you to draw your bills on him direct. If you cannot persuade him to open a credit in your favour in London you may agree to do this, even if he has not arranged for a London bank to negotiate your bills (see method three above) under authority from his own bank.

You draw your bills on your overseas customer and take them, with documents attached, to your own bankers, the Lombard Bank.

The Lombard Bank will do one of three things for you. Either (*a*) they will buy the bills from you; or (*b*) they will make you an advance, against the security of the bills; or (*c*) they will simply handle the bills for collection through their overseas correspondents, but will neither buy them nor make an advance against them. Let us study each of these three courses of action by your bankers:

a – *The Lombard Bank buys the bills from you:* If your bank agree to buy these bills from you (or to make you an advance against them) it is largely on the strength of your good name that they do so, and it is to you as the drawer of the bills that the bank will have recourse for payment if for any reason your overseas client fails to pay on the due date.

The price which the bank will pay you for a bill drawn in £ will vary with current money rates. If the bill is drawn in foreign currency the Lombard Bank, provided they are at the time buyers of that particular currency, will pay you at their current buying rate for drafts on the country of the drawee. In either case, in fixing the price at which they will buy your bill, the bank will include a provision for their own handling charges and for those of their overseas correspondents, who will present the bill to the drawee for acceptance and later for payment by him at maturity. Meanwhile you have had the advantage of being paid cash for your shipment.

This procedure, you will note, is the reverse of that described on page 45 under the heading of 'Negotiated (trade) bill', which concerns importers and import bills. However, bills drawn by exporters on their overseas customers, and passed through London bankers for acceptance abroad, are not 'bills on London' and they are not dealt in on the London discount market. Even if they were drawn 'payable in London' they would still be classed as foreign domicile bills.

An example of a foreign domicile bill appears on the next page at fig 4. See also: 'foreign domicile bills', page 23, and 'The negotiated bill', page 36.

b – *The Lombard Bank make you an advance, against the security of the bills:* In this case when you take the bills, with documents attached, to the Lombard Bank, the bank, by previous agreement, make you a cash advance, at current

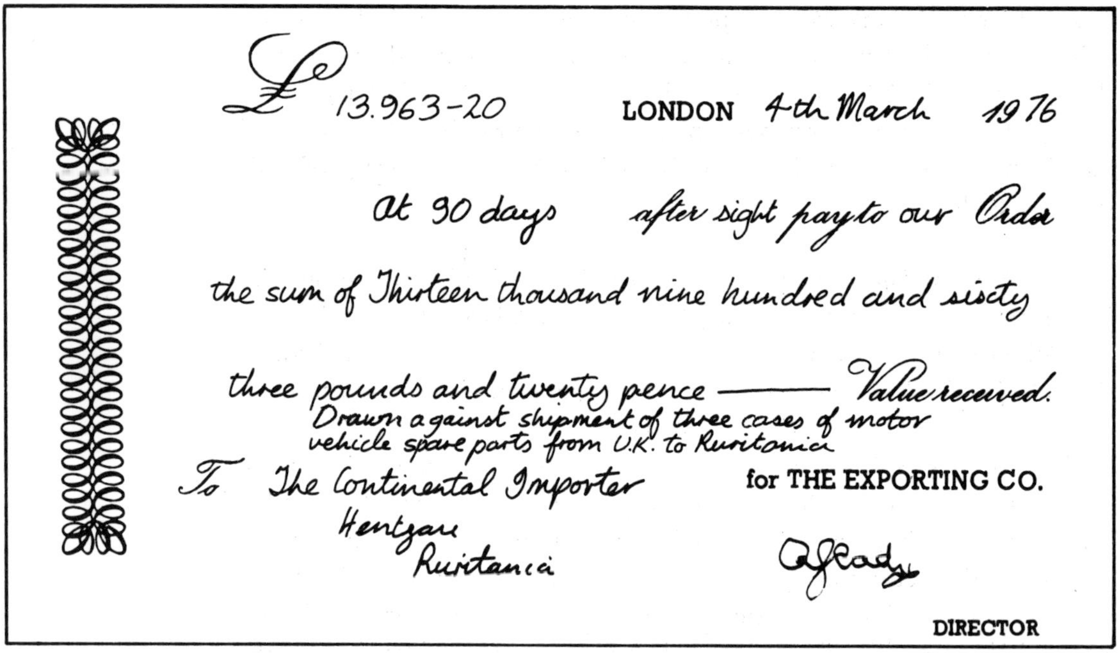

£ 13.963–20   LONDON 4th March   19 76

At 90 days   after sight pay to our Order

the sum of Thirteen thousand nine hundred and sixty

three pounds and twenty pence ———— Value received.
Drawn against shipment of three cases of motor
vehicle spare parts from U.K. to Ruritania

To   The Continental Importer   for THE EXPORTING CO.
     Hentzau
        Ruritania   DIRECTOR

FIGURE 4
An export bill drawn by The Exporting Co, London, on the Continental Importer,
Hentzau (foreign domicile) as described on the previous page.

*This bill does not appear again in the book as there is no mention of foreign domicile bills in part three
(Procedure), and it is not suitable for inclusion in the parcel of bills.*

advance rates, of say 80% of the face value of the bills. The bank then forward the bills to their overseas correspondents for presentation to the drawee for acceptance, and later for payment. When in due course your overseas customer pays the bills at maturity the Lombard Bank credit you with the proceeds, and your advance is paid off. The Lombard Bank will debit you for their handling charges, and for those of their overseas correspondents, and will pay to you the balance remaining from the margin of 20% of the face value of the bills.

c – *The Lombard Bank may only be prepared to handle the bills for collection:* The Lombard Bank may not be willing either to buy these foreign domicile bills from you, or to make you an advance against them. Their willingness to do so depends largely on your own credit standing, but to some extent also on their assessment of the standing of the drawee and of the political, economic, and foreign exchange factors ruling in the country to which you are consigning your goods.

Whatever the reason, if the bank are not willing to buy your bills, or to make you an advance against them, they will simply handle them for you, in accordance with The International Chamber of Commerce Uniform Rules for the Collection of Commercial Paper, sending them out to their overseas correspondents for presentation to the drawee for acceptance, and again at maturity for payment, thus collecting the proceeds for your account. For these services the bank will make you a handling charge which may include the charges of their overseas banking correspondents.

II THE BILL OF EXCHANGE AND THE IMPORTER
TO THE IMPORTING COMPANY

You are an importer of commodities. Your overseas exporter, The Wool-buying Co, Atlantis, stipulates payment against shipment, or against the shipping documents. Unless you use a term bill this means that you will be out of your money for the period the goods are in transit and probably for longer. There are a number of methods by which the bill of exchange may help you.

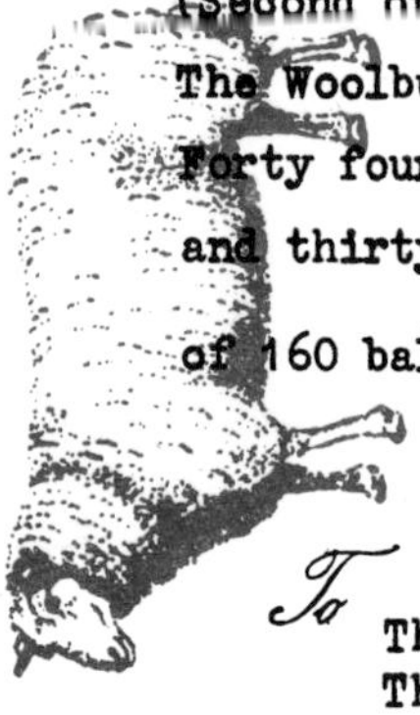

EXCHANGE FOR £44,388 - 39   Royal City, Atlantis 8th April *19* 76

At 90 days sight   *pay this* first *Bill of Exchange*

(Second of same tenor and date being unpaid)   *to the Order of*

The Woolbuying Co ------------------------------------ the sum of

Forty four thousand three hundred and eighty eight pounds

and thirty nine pence.   Drawn under Credit I.C. 7929 against shipment

of 160 bales of wool from Atlantis to U.K. per SS " GOLDEN FLEECE".

For and on behalf of
THE WOOLBUYING CO.

To The Lombard Bank,
Threadneedle Street,
London,
E.C.2.

JDolby.

Director

FIGURE 5
An import bill drawn by The Woolbuying Co of Atlantis on the Lombard Bank, London,
under an irrevocable documentary credit as described on the opposite page.

The same bill, accepted by the Lombard Bank and endorsed by The Woolbuying Co, will be found at
fig 5a in part three (Procedure) on p 76, and again in the parcel of bills at the end of the book.

METHOD A: *The irrevocable documentary letter of credit (in favour of The Overseas Exporter)*

You can ask your banker, the Lombard Bank, or an accepting house, to open an irrevocable documentary letter of credit in favour of the overseas seller (for a specimen request see p 74). Let us say that you make your request to the Lombard Bank, and that they agree to act for you in this way.

The Lombard Bank will issue, through their agents in the country of the exporter, the Bank of Atlantis, Atlantis, a letter of credit in favour of the exporter. In this letter the Lombard Bank will undertake to accept a term bill of exchange drawn on them by the exporter, provided the bill is accompanied by all the correct shipping documents relating to the goods.

The exporter draws the bill on the Lombard Bank (see fig 5 opposite) and hands it, with documents attached, to his local bank which buys the bill from him for cash. His bank, which may be the Bank of Atlantis or some other bank, then forward the bill and the documents to their London correspondents for presentation to the Lombard Bank for acceptance, and the documents are surrendered to the Lombard Bank against their acceptance of the bill.

The Lombard Bank will release the documents to you against payment of the amount of the bill, or they may by special arrangement be prepared to release them to you in trust in advance of payment, so that you can obtain delivery of the goods. In any event, at or before maturity of the bill, you will have to put the Lombard Bank in funds to meet it, but by that time, in most cases, you will have sold the goods and will have the funds available.

Specimen of the letter of credit issued by the Lombard Bank through their overseas agent, the Bank of Atlantis, will be found on page 75.

METHOD B: *London acceptance credit (in favour of the importer)*

You learn, or are advised by a discount house, that Messrs William Caxton & Co, are willing to grant facilities for your type of business. You therefore go to William Caxton and ask them to open an acceptance credit in your favour. This, on the basis of your good name and of the figures you show them, they agree to do. You arrange the details of the credit and these are put in writing in the form of an acceptance credit facility signed by William

£25,000 -00 ------------ BRADFORD   5th April, *19* **76**

At 3 months *after* sight *pay to* the *Order*

of The Importing Co. ------------------------------- the sum of

Twenty Five thousand pounds------------------------*Value received.*

Drawn under Credit No.S2196 against part of shipment of 1,000 bales of
wool from Royal City, Atlantis, to the United Kingdom per S.S. "GOLDEN
FLEECE".

for THE IMPORTING CO.

To William Caxton & Co.,
London, E.C.2.

W. Laurie

DIRECTOR

The Importing Company
BRADFORD

FIGURE 6

An import bill drawn by The Importing Co on William Caxton & Co, London, under a
London acceptance credit, as described on the opposite page.

*The same bill, accepted by William Caxton & Co and endorsed by The Importing Co, will be found at
fig 6a in part three (Procedure) on p 81, and again in the parcel of bills at the end of the book.*

Caxton, who thereby agree that they will accept bills drawn on them by you, subject to the stated conditions. You sign the appropriate form of agreement and undertaking.

When you are due to make payment to your overseas supplier, The Wool-buying Co, Atlantis, you will draw a bill at say three months sight on William Caxton. You send them the bill for acceptance and, at the same time, in your covering letter, you instruct them to pass it to a discount house for discount. You send a copy of this letter to the discount house, with instructions to them to pay the proceeds of the discount to your bankers, the Lombard Bank. The money now being with the Lombard Bank you are able to send a remittance to the exporter in payment for the goods. Three months later, when the bill falls due, you will have to put William Caxton in funds to meet it.

Whether William Caxton will require security for granting the facility is a matter for negotiation. In normal times, and for borrowers of the highest standing, accepting houses are willing to offer 'clean' facilities.

Alternatively, instead of undertaking to remit the funds to The Wool-buying Co you may have agreed with them that they will draw a bill on you at sight. They will probably negotiate this bill through their own bankers, who will forward it to London where it will be presented to you with documents attached, and you will have to pay it in cash. To obtain the funds you will simultaneously draw a term bill of your own on William Caxton under an acceptance credit which they have previously agreed to open in your favour, and you will discount the bill in London. This credit too may be on a 'clean' basis, but it is more likely that William Caxton will require you to deposit the shipping documents with them under a letter of hypothecation. Later, if they consider your standing sufficiently good, they may release the documents to you in trust, as mentioned under method A.

An example of the bill which you would draw in either case appears opposite at fig 6.

See also specimen letters of credit issued to you, an importer, by William Caxton & Co.

(i)   granting unsecured facilities, on page 78.

(ii) requiring security, on page 79.

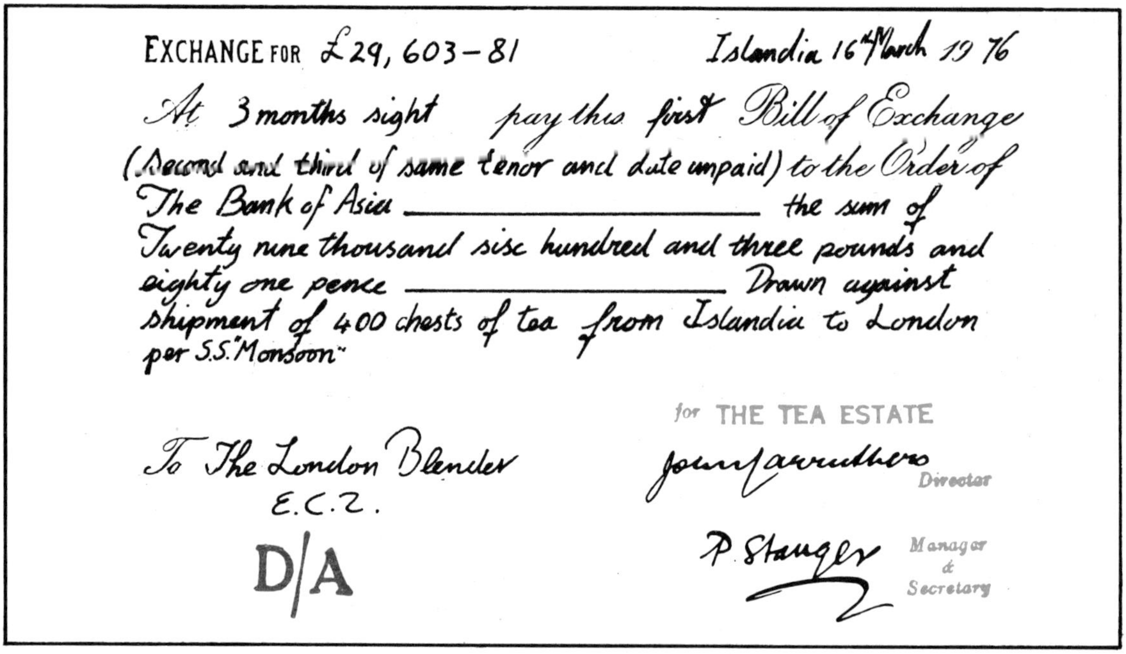

EXCHANGE FOR £29,603-81   Islandia 16th March 1976

At 3 months sight   pay this first Bill of Exchange (Second and third of same tenor and date unpaid) to the Order of The Bank of Asia _____ the sum of Twenty nine thousand six hundred and three pounds and eighty one pence _____ Drawn against shipment of 400 chests of tea from Islandia to London per S.S. "Monsoon"

To The London Blender
E.C.2.

D/A

for THE TEA ESTATE
John Carruthers   Director

P. Stanger   Manager & Secretary

FIGURE 7

An import bill drawn by The Tea Estate, Islandia, on The London Blender, London, for negotiation through the Bank of Asia, as described on pages 45 and 46.

This bill, accepted by The London Blender, and endorsed by The Bank of Asia, London, will be found in the parcel of bills at the end of the book.

METHOD C: *The negotiated (trade) bill*

TO THE LONDON BLENDER (IMPORTER OF TEA)

You, an importer, may arrange with your overseas seller that he shall draw bills *on you* for his shipments of goods, in fulfilment of your orders. This arrangement is traditional for British imports from the far east, and it is equally applicable to imports from other parts of the world. You, for example, are a London tea blender, and you procure your tea in Islandia, from 'The Tea Estate'. They want immediate payment for their shipments, but you do not wish to pay for the tea until it reaches London, or until some time later.

You ask the Bank of Asia, London, to authorise their Islandia office to negotiate bills drawn on you by The Tea Estate in £ sterling, at say 90 days sight, to cover the c.i.f. value of a shipment of a definite number of chests of tea. The Tea Estate draw a bill on you and present it, with all the relative shipping documents attached, to the Islandia branch of the Bank of Asia, who negotiate it, i.e. buy it, from The Tea Estate at the bank's buying rate of exchange for 90 days sight drafts on London. The bank pay The Tea Estate in local currency, and forward the bill and the documents to the Bank of Asia, London.

The Bank of Asia, London, present the bill to you, The London Blender, for your acceptance, and then hold it, with the documents, until you pay it.

Meanwhile, The Tea Estate having been paid in Islandia, the chests of tea are on their way across the seas to London, and you do not have to pay for them until the bill falls due. If, however, you wish to obtain earlier delivery of the tea you may pay the bill before maturity, and in that case you will be allowed a rebate on the bill amount.

If you do not wish to take delivery before maturity of the bill, the Bank of Asia, on arrival of the steamer, will see that the tea is stored in an approved tea warehouse. You as the acceptor of the bill are entitled to name the warehouse you prefer, and you will have to provide adequate insurance cover on which the bank will require a lien. All landing charges and warehouse and other charges will be payable by you.

It may be that by reason of your good credit standing you will be able to arrange d/a (documents against acceptance) terms. This means that the Bank of Asia will deliver the shipping documents to you against your acceptance of the bill. In this case the Bank of Asia, London, will hold the bill, accepted by you, in their own portfolio, and they may then, when it suits them to do so, endorse the bill and sell it to a London discount house.

This is a very brief description of the financing of a single shipment of one commodity, chosen only as an example. It will be understood that the expert knowledge of the banks and accepting houses, as well as of the shippers, merchants, warehouse companies and others concerned will produce a great variety of solutions for the many different problems which arise in international trade.

An example of a negotiated bill, covering the import of tea from Islandia to the UK, appears on page 44 at fig 7.

NOTE ON BANK ENDORSED BILLS

If the Bank of Asia decide not to hold the bill until maturity, but to sell it to a London discount house, they may endorse it, and thus make it, from the discount market's point of view, a 'bank endorsed bill'. As such it may be included by the Bank of Asia in a mixed parcel of bills which they will sell to a discount house, with a variety of drawers and acceptors, and covering shipments of several different commodities.

These bills will all be very acceptable to the discount house because all will bear the endorsement of the Bank of Asia, and bills which carry the endorsement of a London bank can be of just as fine quality as those accepted by a London bank, since the endorsement is in effect a guarantee that if for any reason the acceptor and the drawer both fail to meet the bill at maturity the bank, as endorser, will do so.

III   THE BILL OF EXCHANGE AND THE MANUFACTURER

TO THE BRITISH MANUFACTURER

One of your problems is to finance your purchases of raw materials required in your factory, from the time when you have to pay for them until you receive payment for the finished product. The balance of this finance that your own resources will not meet is normally provided by bank advance.

Equally, it is possible to borrow a part of the money on bills of exchange to cover the period during which the raw materials are on their way to the factory, or waiting in the warehouse, or passing through the processes of manufacture. For borrowers of high credit standing, London accepting houses are usually prepared to grant acceptance facilities for that purpose.

For instance, you may have to make seasonal purchases of some months' supply of raw materials for your factory. For these you have to pay all at once, and then for several months you are working on them and turning them into finished goods. You discuss your problem with a well-known accepting house, Messrs William Caxton & Co, who agree to grant you a credit. You then draw your bills at, say, 90 days sight on William Caxton, who accept them, and, on your instructions, hand them for discount to a discount house. The discount house pays the net proceeds into your account at 'The Lombard Bank'. On the maturity of the bills you will have to put William Caxton in funds to meet them. This may, by agreement, be done by your drawing and discounting a new set of bills and paying the proceeds to William Caxton to meet the bills falling due. In theory the 90 days is the approximate interval between paying for the raw materials and receiving proceeds of sale of the made up article, and the assumption is that by maturity of one set of bills you will be ready to take up fresh raw materials, thus justifying the drawing of new bills.

This procedure can be repeated so long as the facility remains open. Subject to the limit of the credit, variations in the amount of the accommodation required are provided for by drawing a larger or smaller total of bills on renewal. As we have said on page 26, bills of this type are sometimes classified as 'finance bills' but much depends on the nature of the trade.

A specimen facility letter issued in your favour for the financing of purchases of raw materials, by Messrs William Caxton & Co, will be found on page 86.

A specimen bill appears on page 48 at fig 8.

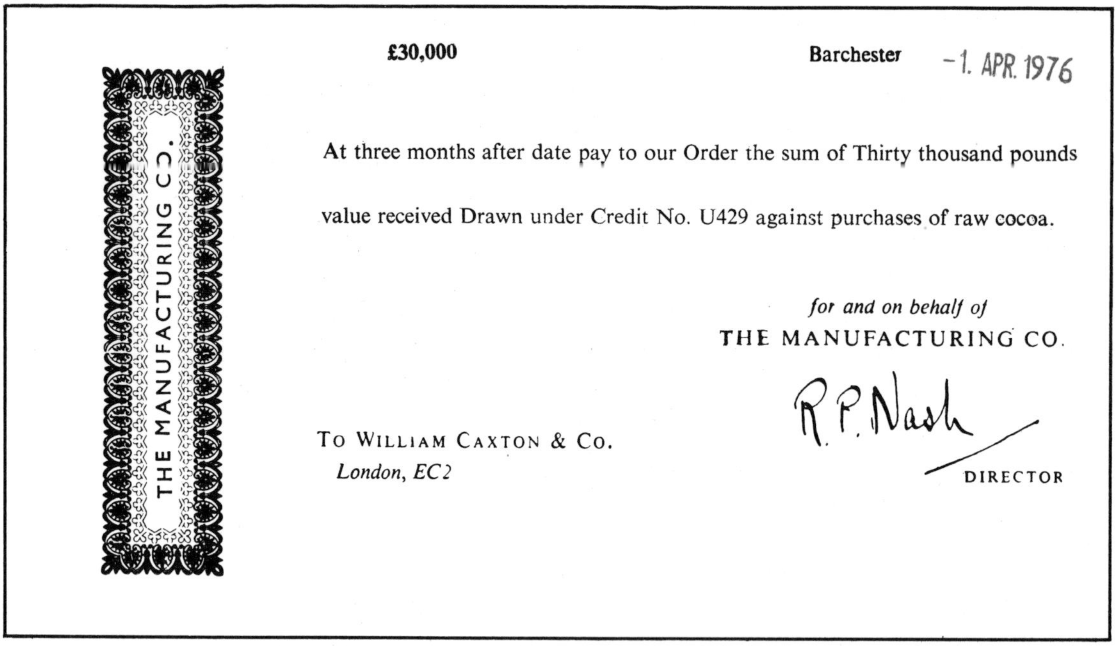

£30,000   Barchester   – 1. APR. 1976

THE MANUFACTURING CO.

At three months after date pay to our Order the sum of Thirty thousand pounds

value received Drawn under Credit No. U429 against purchases of raw cocoa.

for and on behalf of
THE MANUFACTURING CO.

R. P. Nash

DIRECTOR

To WILLIAM CAXTON & CO.
London, EC2

FIGURE 8
A manufacturer's bill drawn by The Manufacturing Co, Barchester, on William Caxton
& Co, under an acceptance credit, as described on page 47.

The same bill, accepted by William Caxton & Co, and endorsed by The Manufacturing Co, will be
found at fig 8a in part three (Procedure) on p 88, and again in the parcel of bills at the end of the book.

IV TRADE BILLS

TO THE BRITISH TRADER IN GOODS FOR SALE TO INDUSTRY IN
THE UK

You may be in a business in which it is customary for you, the seller of the goods, to draw bills of exchange direct on your customers, who are buying the goods from you. A bill so drawn is known as a 'trade bill'. *(See fig 9 on page 50.)*

Trade bills are well recognised in the discount market, though they are not so readily negotiable as are bank bills, and they do not command the same fine rates. This is of little importance when you are not in need of the money, and are therefore content to hold the accepted trade bills until maturity. If, however, you wish to have the money at once, or at any time before the bills fall due, you can offer the bills for discount either to your own bankers or to a discount house. Your normal outlet for trade bills is with your bankers, who have intimate knowledge of your business, but some of these bills can be placed in the discount market.

The rate which a bank or discount house will quote you for a trade bill will depend on their assessment of a number of factors. In brief, you will normally get a keen quotation for your trade bills if both you and your customer enjoy good credit standing, if the trade against which the bills are drawn is considered suitable for finance by means of bills, and if there is not already in circulation too great a volume of trade bills and especially of trade bills carrying your name or that of your customer or covering the same type of goods as those in which you are dealing. Trade bills which could be described as pure finance bills (see p 26) would not be well received.

There is an element of uncertainty in the ability to discount any large amount of trade bills, and this could be a serious disadvantage to a seller of goods who requires immediate cash. For this reason many leading business concerns prefer to incur the small additional expense of opening acceptance credits with London bankers. They thus ensure that the bills they draw will always be saleable in the discount market at a fine rate.

You yourself as a trader, drawing a substantial amount of trade bills on good customers, in the normal course of your business, might find that an

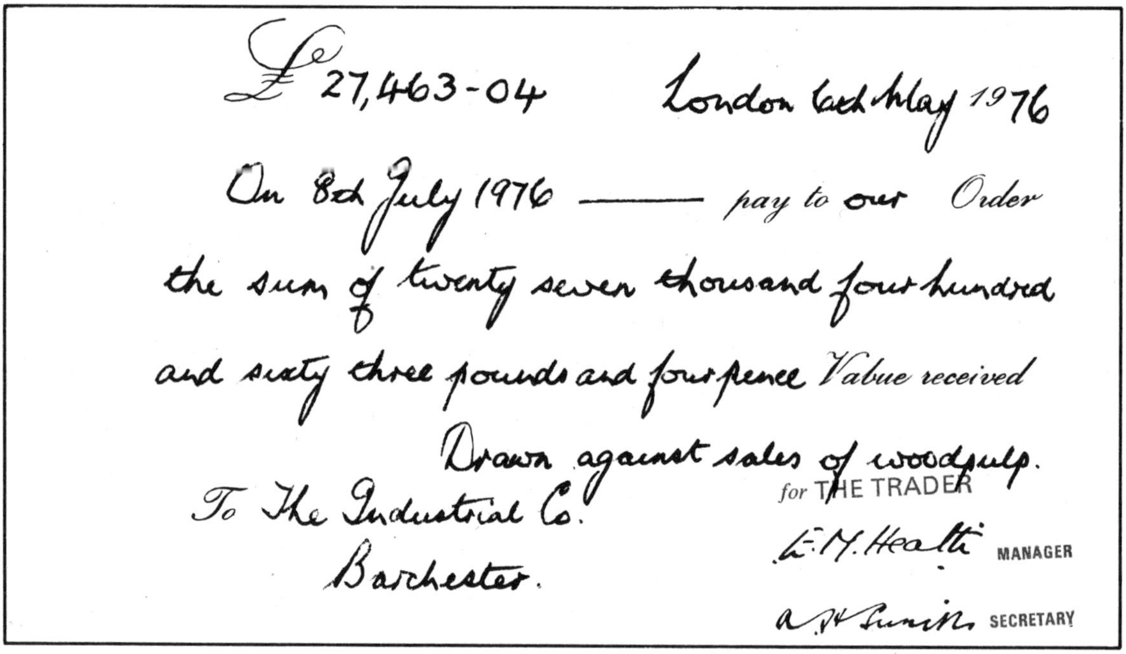

£ 27,463-04   London 6th May 1976

On 8th July 1976 ——— pay to our   Order

the sum of twenty seven thousand four hundred

and sixty three pounds and fourpence *Value received*

Drawn against sales of woodpulp.

To The Industrial Co.
Barchester.

for THE TRADER

E. M. Heath MANAGER

A. H. Smith SECRETARY

FIGURE 9
A trade bill drawn by The Trader, London, on The Industrial Co, Barchester, as described on page 49.

This bill, accepted by The Industrial Co and endorsed by the Trader, will be found in the parcel of bills at the end of this book.

accepting house would be willing to grant you an acceptance credit secured by the deposit of some of your trade bills. The accepting house would require to be satisfied with the credit standing both of yourself and of the customers on whom you were drawing your bills, and the amount of the trade bills which you put up as security would have to exceed the amount of your own drawings against these bills by a margin agreed between you and the accepting house.

A credit of this kind would not greatly differ from that outlined under 'The bill of exchange and the exporter, method two, London acceptance credit', page 33. See also part three (Procedure), pages 68–73.

V THE BILL OF EXCHANGE AND THE INTERNATIONAL TRADER

TO THE INTERNATIONAL TRADER

You are a British trader dealing with the purchase, shipment and sale of goods and commodities in various parts of the world. You deal not only in imports and exports of Great Britain, but also in shipments which never touch the shores of these islands. You may need to be able to borrow money rapidly and easily when, as often happens, the money you are due to receive from one end of the world does not coincide with the money you are having to pay to the other.

Banks and accepting houses in the City of London are normally prepared to issue letters of credit to, or on behalf of, international traders like yourself.

When you are acting as a buyer you may obtain bill finance just as an importer does, even though the goods you are buying may be going direct to some other foreign country and may never come to the UK. You may arrange credits in the manner outlined under the heading 'The bill of exchange and the importer, method A, irrevocable documentary letter of credit', page 41. In this case the exporter will be the drawer of the bills. Alternatively you may arrange credit facilities for yourself with a London bank or accepting house on the lines of 'The bill of exchange and the importer, method B, London acceptance credit', page 41, in which case you will draw the bills on the bank or accepting house and discount them in the London discount market.

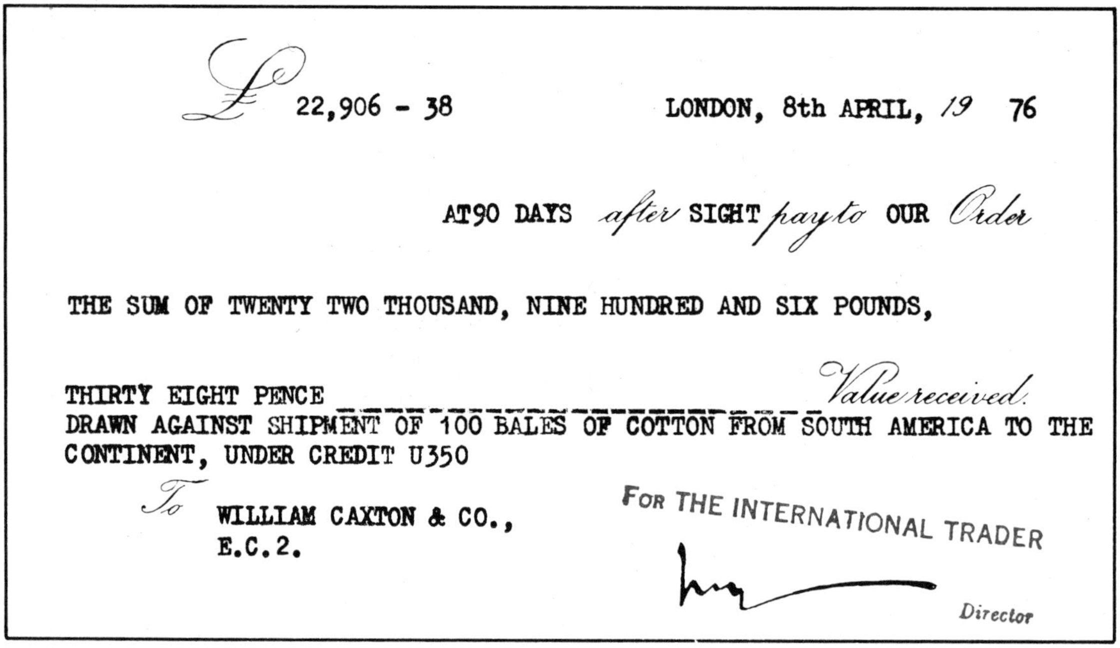

£ 22,906 - 38   LONDON, 8th APRIL, *19* 76

AT 90 DAYS *after* SIGHT *pay to* OUR *Order*

THE SUM OF TWENTY TWO THOUSAND, NINE HUNDRED AND SIX POUNDS,

THIRTY EIGHT PENCE _____ *Value received.*
DRAWN AGAINST SHIPMENT OF 100 BALES OF COTTON FROM SOUTH AMERICA TO THE
CONTINENT, UNDER CREDIT U350

To   WILLIAM CAXTON & CO.,   FOR THE INTERNATIONAL TRADER
       E.C.2.

                                              Director

FIGURE 10

An International trader's bill drawn by The International Trader, London, on William
Caxton & Co. London, under an acceptance credit as described on pages 51 and 53.

*This bill, accepted by William Caxton & Co. and endorsed by The International Trader, will be
found in the parcel of bills at the end of the book.*

When you are acting as a seller or exporter it will usually be the buyer or importer who will arrange for a credit, preferably an irrevocable credit, to be opened in your favour through a London bank or accepting house in which case you will draw the bill and sell it for cash in the London discount market (see 'The bill of exchange and the exporter, method one, irrevocable documentary letter of credit', page 31). Alternatively you may arrange credit facilities for yourself with a London bank or accepting house on the lines of 'The bill of exchange and the exporter, method two, London acceptance credit', page 33, in which case again you will draw the bills on the bank or accepting house and discount them in the London discount market.

You may thus, with your varied business, have occasion to draw bills on London under a number of different credits. You will find it will be of value to you to have direct dealings with a London discount house, so that you may have a regular outlet for your bills, and a source of information and advice on all matters concerning the London bill market.

A specimen bill, drawn by you on Messrs William Caxton & Co, a London accepting house, under a credit opened by them in your favour, appears on the opposite page at fig 10.

VI REMITTED BILLS

THE BILL ON LONDON AND THE FOREIGN BANKER

You are the foreign manager of the Bank of Europa whose head office is on the Continent, with no branch in London. Many of your customers are engaged in overseas trade and they discuss with you how their business can be financed. If you wish to arrange finance for them in sterling in London you will find that there are a number of ways in which the bill on London can help you, assuming that any necessary approval is forthcoming from the Exchange Control authorities in your country and in the United Kingdom.

A—FINANCING EXPORTS

(i) The irrevocable documentary letter of credit

Your customer is exporting finished goods to The Overseas Importer, Newtown, Atlantis, who is asking for credit. If the conditions of the market permit, the best procedure is to request The Overseas Importer to open in favour of your customer an irrevocable documentary letter of credit with a London bank. Acting on behalf of your customer you will send the bill and documents called for under the credit, to the London bank, with instructions that after accepting the bill the bank should hand it to a discount house for discount. At the same time you will ask the discount house to pay the proceeds to your London correspondents for the credit of your account. An example of this type of credit is given under 'The bill of exchange and the exporter', method one, on page 31, the only difference being that instead of the British exporter being the beneficiary of the credit your customer will be the beneficiary and you will be acting on his behalf.

(ii) London acceptance credit

You, as a foreign bank of good standing, will have direct connections with a London accepting house, for example, William Caxton & Co. If so, you may ask William Caxton for a line of credit, under which they would allow your customers to draw on them bills to the extent of the credit, in connection with their export business. These bills would bear your endorsement and would be accepted for your account. William Caxton & Co would probably require evidence of the business your customers were doing, and might make it a condition that bills drawn by your customers on the overseas importers, together with the documents of title to the goods, should be handled by them. Out of the collections William Caxton & Co would obtain the funds to meet the bills drawn on them by your customers, crediting any balances to your account. When you send the bills drawn on William Caxton & Co to them for acceptance, you would request them to hand the bills to a discount house for discount. At the same time you would ask the discount house to pay the proceeds of the discount to your London correspondents for the credit of your account. This type of credit is illustrated in 'The bill of exchange and the exporter', method two, page 33, the only differences being that the credit is opened in favour of your customers, and that they draw the bills under your responsibility.

B—FINANCING IMPORTS

One of your customers, The Continental Importer, wishes to import a consignment of spices from the far east. The seller of the spices demands payment in the far east in sterling at the time of shipment. Your customer, on the other hand, does not wish to put up the cash until the consignment has reached his own city. There are two principal ways in which the bill on London may be used to help with the finance, assuming again that any necessary approval is forthcoming from the Exchange Control authorities in your country and in the United Kingdom.

(i) Credit opened in London in favour of the exporter

One way is for you to ask your London correspondents, the Lombard Bank, to open a credit in favour of the exporter in the far east, who will then draw a bill on the Lombard Bank. You will put up the necessary funds when the bill reaches maturity and arrange for your own reimbursement from your customer.

(ii) Credit opened in London on your responsibility in favour of your customer

As a foreign banker of good standing you can ask one of your London correspondents, for example the Lombard Bank, to make payment on your behalf to the shipper in the far east, alternatively, to pay a sight bill drawn on them by the shipper in the far east, against production of the documents. Then, by agreement already made between you and the Lombard Bank you instruct your customer, The Continental Importer, to draw a bill on the Lombard Bank. This bill you endorse and send to the Lombard Bank for acceptance. You may ask the Lombard Bank to arrange the discount of the bill or, if you are in direct touch with a London discount house, you may request the Lombard Bank to hand the bill to them for discount. The proceeds of the discount are paid to the Lombard Bank who are thus reimbursed for the remittance they have made to the far east. The Lombard Bank send the shipping documents to you for release to your customer in accordance with the arrangements you have made with him. You are responsible to the Lombard Bank for putting them in funds to meet the bill drawn on them by your customer when it matures.

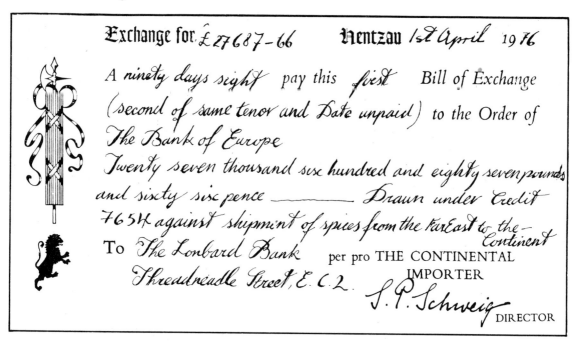

Exchange for £27687–66   Hentzau 1st April 1976

A *ninety days sight* pay this *first* Bill of Exchange
(second of same tenor and Date unpaid) to the Order of
The Bank of Europe
Twenty seven thousand six hundred and eighty seven pounds
and sixty six pence ——————— Drawn under Credit
76514 against shipment of spices from the FarEast to the
                                                Continent
To The Lombard Bank   per pro THE CONTINENTAL
    Threadneedle Street, E.C.2   IMPORTER
                            J.P. Schweig
                                        DIRECTOR

FIGURE 11

A continental importer's bill, drawn by The Continental Importer, Hentzau, on the
Lombard Bank, London, under a credit arranged by the Bank of Europa.

*This bill, endorsed by the Bank of Europa, accepted by the Lombard Bank, and discounted in London,
is a remitted bill as described on p. 53. It will be found in the parcel of bills at the end of the book.*

This method is frequently referred to as the 're-finance credit'. The extent to which these credits have been permitted in the United Kingdom has been subject to restriction, in varying degree, by Exchange Control regulation.

An example of a bill drawn on London, under a credit opened with a London bank by a foreign bank, and remitted to London for acceptance and discount appears on the opposite page at Fig. 11.

THE BILL ON LONDON AND THE CONTINENTAL MERCHANT
As a continental merchant of good standing, you may have direct connections with a London accepting house, for example William Caxton & Co. If so, you can arrange to finance your trade using the bill on London in the same way as described in the last section. The only difference is that the credits opened by you will not be arranged through the Bank of Europa but on your behalf and on your responsibility.

VII   A PARCEL OF BILLS
It may be of interest to hear what happens to a bill after it has been drawn, accepted by a bank or accepting house, and subsequently discounted with a discount house. This then is the sequence of events if a bill is discounted with us, Gillett Brothers Discount Company Ltd.

First, we have discounted (i.e. looking at it from our side, bought) the bill and it is now our property and is held in what we call our 'case', or 'portfolio' of bills. This particular bill is a bank bill, drawn on William Caxton & Co. We enter the details of the bill in our records and forthwith put it out as security against a loan from one of the banks, who are accustomed to leave with the discount market a proportion of their liquid funds. We hope the rate of interest we are paying for the loan will remain less than the rate of discount at which we bought the bill, because this is where we reckon to earn a good part of our profit.

Alternatively, we may sell the bill to someone who is looking for an investment for liquid funds. The largest buyers of bills from us have traditionally been the clearing banks, who have considered them just about the finest liquid investment they could have. Other holders of liquid funds have also

PARCEL No. K219

AMOUNT £	DRAWER	ACCEPTOR	ENDORSER	DUE DATE 1976
65,391.40	The Exporting Co.	*The Bank of Atlantis*	The Exporting Co.	14 June
36,000.00	The Exporting Co.	*Wm. Caxton & Co.*	The Exporting Co.	21 June
29,603.81	The Tea Estate	*The London Blender*	The Bank of Asia	25 June
30,000.00	The Manufacturing Co.	*Wm. Caxton & Co.*	The Manufacturing Co.	1 July
27,687.66	The Continental Importer	*The Lombard Bank*	The Bank of Europa	5 July
25,000.00	The Importing Co.	*Wm. Caxton & Co.*	The Importing Co.	6 July
22,906.38	The International Trader	*Wm. Caxton & Co.*	The International Trader	7 July
27,463.04	The Trader	*The Industrial Co.*	The Trader	8 July
44,388.39	The Woolbuying Co.	*The Lombard Bank*	The Woolbuying Co.	12 July
£308,440.68	TOTAL			

seen their attractions.

The bill of exchange as an investment is described in the next chapter.

The bills which we have described and illustrated in these pages would be regarded as suitable to secure a loan from a bank. On this page will be found the list of bills and replicas of the bills will be found, made up as a parcel, at the end of the book.

VIII   THE BILL OF EXCHANGE AND THE INVESTOR

You are a holder of funds which you wish to invest for a short period. One of the investments you can make is to buy bills of exchange at a discount on the amounts they will realise at maturity (their face value). Before buying you will wish to consider what return you will receive on the money you are investing, how long it will be before you get your money back, and how safe it is.

A – THE RETURN

When a bill changes hands, the return on it is expressed as a discount of so much per cent per annum. No commission is payable if it is bought from a discount house. The discount rate will depend on market factors at the time, and also on the particular bill which is being purchased and its quality (see part one, V THE QUALITY OF A BILL, p 22). In comparing the rate of discount quoted for a bill with the rate of interest quoted for a deposit of money, it must be remembered that if the rates quoted are the same, then the return obtainable from buying the bill is higher than that obtainable from depositing the money. This is because the discount charge is deducted from the amount you originally invest, whereas you will not receive interest on your deposit until it is repaid. The difference is small for short periods and when rates are low, but becomes more appreciable when the period is longer and/or interest rates are higher.

See note on discount rates, page 62.

B – THE PERIOD

Bills are most commonly drawn to mature in three months or 90 days, so that you should not count on being able to invest in bills for longer periods. If you have money to invest for shorter periods you will usually be able to find bills maturing on a suitable date, not only because bills may be drawn for shorter periods, but because a discount house is likely to be able to offer bills which it has been holding.

C – SAFETY

The buyer of a bill becomes its holder, and all previous parties to the bill –

acceptor, drawer and endorser(s) if any – are legally responsible for its payment under the provisions of the Bills of Exchange Act, 1882. The parties to a bill are described on page 15, and their several rights and responsibilities are defined in the glossary at the end of the book.

The safety of an investment in a bill will therefore be judged primarily by the names of the parties to it. The nature of the transaction against which it is drawn is also considered. These aspects are discussed in part one, V.

A point of interest to the investor is that when he buys from a discount house he is buying an investment that the discount house was itself prepared to hold; and that in the case of sterling bills the discount house will endorse those he buys, and so guarantee their payment at maturity.

IX   CONCLUSION

This brief outline of some of the traditional uses of the bill will, we hope, have given the reader some idea of the flexibility of the bill on London, which serves so many trades in all parts of the world, with so many variations of technique.

Bills are perfectly suited for the finance of the movement of goods, and there are few financial problems in world trade to which they cannot be adapted.

The market in bills is made by the discount houses, who by tradition and long practice have made themselves expert in all matters connected with bills.

The advice of the City of London on all problems of finance is available to any firm requiring it. To get the complete picture a firm should be in close touch with its own bankers, its own accepting house, and its own discount house.

Part three
Procedure

'There are nine and sixty ways
of constructing tribal lays,
And every single one of them is right.'

NOTES

I – ACCEPTING COMMISSION

The rates of accepting commission quoted for the specimen credits shown in the following pages are only examples. The level of rates varies, and the actual charge made by the bank or accepting house is a matter for negotiation in each case.

2 – DISCOUNT RATES

The discount rates quoted in the discount statements are given only as examples, for the sake of making the procedure clear.

The cost in terms of interest of discounting a bill if you are a seller, or the yield if you are a buyer of a bill, can be calculated by use of the following formula:

$$\frac{\text{Discount} \times 365 \times 100}{\text{Sum received or invested} \times \text{number of days}}$$

The relative rate of interest for the discounter on page 85 would be:

$$\frac{9{,}006.51 \times 365 \times 100}{415{,}993.49 \times 91} = 8.684\%, \text{ equivalent to a discount rate of } 8\tfrac{1}{2}\%$$

3 – CREDITS

The wording of the letters granting the facilities will vary amongst banks but in the case of documentary letters of credit, standard forms are available in conformity with 'Uniform Customs and Practice for Documentary Credits' (1974 Revision) International Chamber of Commerce (Publication No. 290).

1   THE BILL OF EXCHANGE AND THE EXPORTER

(See part two, pp. 31–39)

Here is an example of the letter of credit which an exporter will receive from a bank or accepting house when with his concurrence his customer, The Overseas Importer, arranges for an irrevocable documentary letter of credit to be opened in his favour:

1 – *Irrevocable documentary letter of credit issued by a bank or accepting house in favour of the Exporting Company*

BANK OF ATLANTIS, London Office

TO THE EXPORTING COMPANY
London EC2   1 April 1976

Dear Sirs,

At the request of our Newtown branch we wish to advise you that they have opened in your favour an irrevocable documentary letter of credit No. 1162/76, subject to the 'Uniform Customs and Practice for Documentary Credits' (1974 Revision) International Chamber of Commerce (Publication No. 290), under which we will accept bills drawn on us by you at 60 days sight for sums not exceeding in total £66,000 (Sixty-six thousand pounds English currency) on account of The Overseas Importer, Newtown, Atlantis.

Bills drawn under this credit must be accompanied by:

Full set of clean on board bills of lading to shippers' order and endorsed in blank.
Invoice(s).
Insurance policy or certificate for 110% of the approximate CIF value.
evidencing shipment of twenty-five motor vehicles to Atlantis.

This credit expires on 1 July 1976.

Part shipments are allowed.

All bills drawn under this credit must be marked 'Drawn under Bank of Atlantis, Newtown Branch Credit No. 1162/76.'

We hereby undertake to honour all drawings presented to us in accordance with the terms of this credit.

Please note that the stipulations in this credit should be complied with to the letter, as otherwise we may not be able to accept bills drawn under it.

Yours faithfully,
pro Manager   *pro Accountant*

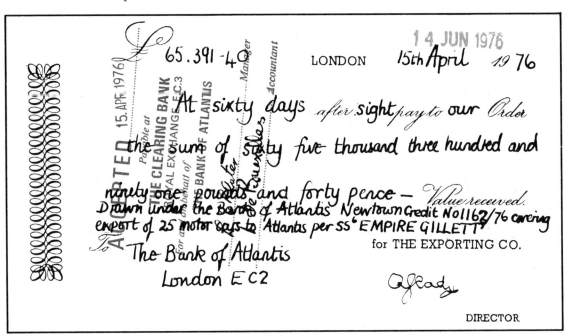

LONDON   15th April   19 76

£ 65.391·40

At sixty days *after sight pay to* our *Order*

the *sum of* sixty five thousand three hundred and

ninety one pounds and forty pence — *Value received.*

Drawn under the Bank of Atlantis Newtown Credit No1162/76 covering

export of 25 motor cars to Atlantis per SS 'EMPIRE GILLETT'

for THE EXPORTING CO.

To The Bank of Atlantis

London E C2

DIRECTOR

For and on behalf of THE EXPORTING CO.

Director.

FIGURE 2a

An export bill (irrevocable documentary letter of credit) – accepted and endorsed.

An example of a bill drawn under this credit appears on the opposite page, fig. 2a.

When all the documents are ready you, The Exporting Company, send them to the Bank of Atlantis, London, together with a bill signed and endorsed, with covering letter as follows:

THE EXPORTING COMPANY, London EC2

TO THE MANAGER

THE BANK OF ATLANTIS

London EC2   15 April 1976

Dear Sir,

Newtown branch credit no. 1162/76

With reference to your letter of 1 April, 1976, we now enclose the following documents covering shipment of twenty-five motor vehicles to Atlantis per S.S. *Empire Gillett*:

Full set of clean on board bills of lading to shippers' order and endorsed in blank
Invoice
Insurance policy

We also enclose our 60-days draft drawn on you for £65,391.40. We should be glad if you would accept this and then hand it to Messrs. Gillett Brothers Discount Company Ltd for discount.

Yours faithfully,

THE EXPORTING COMPANY

At the same time a copy of the above letter should be sent to Gillett Brothers Discount Company Ltd with a covering note as follows:

TO GILLETT BROTHERS DISCOUNT COMPANY LTD

65 Cornhill, London EC3V 3PP   15 April 1976

Dear Sirs,

We enclose a copy of a letter we have to-day sent to the Bank of Atlantis. We should be grateful if you would pay the proceeds of the discount of the bill mentioned in the letter to the Lombard Bank, London EC2, for the credit of our account.

Yours faithfully,

THE EXPORTING COMPANY

Alternatively you may send the bill and documents through your own bankers, with instructions to present the bill to the Bank of Atlantis, and after acceptance to hand it to Gillett Brothers for discounting.

When Gillett Brothers receive the bill from the Bank of Atlantis they will discount it, and in accordance with your instructions pay the proceeds to the Lombard Bank, for the credit of your account. They will then write to you as follows:

GILLETT BROTHERS DISCOUNT COMPANY LTD,
65 Cornhill, London EC3V 3PP

TO THE EXPORTING COMPANY
London EC2   15 April 1976

We have pleasure in confirming the PURCHASE of the bills listed below. In accordance with instructions the net proceeds have been paid to *The Lombard Bank Ltd, EC2, for the credit of your account.*

AMOUNTS	DISCOUNT & PROCEEDS	DUE DATE	NO OF DAYS
65,391.40	65,391.40 $8\frac{1}{2}\%$ 913.69 64,477.71	14 June	60

per pro
GILLETT BROTHERS DISCOUNT COMPANY LTD

If the credit in favour of the exporter had not been opened by the Bank of Atlantis who have a branch in London, but by the Bank of Europa who have no branch in London, the Bank of Europa would ask their London correspondents, the Lombard Bank, to notify the opening of the credit to the exporter and the Lombard Bank would indicate in the notification whether or not they confirmed the credit (see page 33). The clause might read:

Confirmed credit
We confirm the credit, and hereby promise that drafts drawn in accordance with the terms and conditions hereof will be duly honoured on presentation at our office.

Unconfirmed credit
The present advice of the establishment of the credit does not constitute any guarantee or obligation on our part, as we are not instructed to confirm the credit.

Here are examples of facility letters which an exporter might receive from an accepting house:

2 – *Revolving acceptance credit covering exports from the UK to Atlantis opened in favour of the Exporting Company by William Caxton & Co—unsecured.*

WILLIAM CAXTON & CO, London EC2

TO THE EXPORTING COMPANY
London EC2   16 February 1976

Dear Sirs,

Revolving acceptance credit no. U452

With reference to our recent conversations with your representatives we have pleasure in hereby opening for your account a revolving acceptance credit to the extent of:

£400,000 (four hundred thousand pounds sterling) for the purpose of financing your exports of motor vehicles etc. to Atlantis.

The credit is available by your drafts upon ourselves at two or three months sight, which should be enfaced with an indication of the underlying business, such as 'Drawn under credit no. U452 against shipment of . . . to Atlantis'.

All drafts are to be covered by you in cash with us not later than their respective maturity dates, but, the credit being revolving, when and to the extent that drafts have been so covered, the facility of drawing is again open to you within the limits of the credit.

The credit expires on 16 February 1977, that is to say all drafts must be drawn not later than that date. If, however, the facility has worked to our mutual satisfaction, we shall then be glad to consider renewal.

Accepting commission will be at the rate of $1\frac{1}{2}\%$ per annum, i.e. $\frac{1}{4}\%$ on the amounts of drafts at two months sight and $\frac{3}{8}\%$ on amounts of drafts at three months sight.

The credit being unsecured, it is a condition hereof that you will not without our consent create any new mortgage or charge on any of your property or assets.

We enclose our usual form of undertaking* in respect of this credit, which kindly sign and return to us, together with an up-to-date copy of your memorandum and articles of association, copy of a resolution of your board authorising the establishment of the credit, and specimen signatures of those authorised to sign on your behalf in its operation.

Yours faithfully,
WILLIAM CAXTON & CO

* See note on p 70.

3 – *Revolving acceptance credit covering exports from the UK to Atlantis opened in favour of the Exporting Company by William Caxton & Co*—secured.

WILLIAM CAXTON & CO, London EC 2

TO THE EXPORTING COMPANY
London EC 2   16 February 1976

Dear Sirs,

Revolving acceptance credit no. S.3217

In response to your application we have pleasure in placing at your disposal revolving acceptance credit facilities to the extent of:

£400,000 (four hundred thousand pounds)

outstanding at any one time, to assist in the financing of your exports to Atlantis, subject to the following terms and conditions.

This credit is available by your drafts upon ourselves at ninety days or three months sight, which are to be marked 'Drawn under credit No. S.3217 against shipment of . . . to Atlantis'.

At or before time of so drawing upon us, you are to deposit with us, as security, and for collection under our existing arrangements with you, your drafts at usances not exceeding ninety days on your buyers in the importing country, accompanied by full shipping documents, for the underlying goods; the total amount of such drafts is to exceed the respective drawing on us by not less than 15%.

These collections are to be insured by you with the Export Credits Guarantee Department and the relative policies assigned to us, and you are to furnish us with copies of all returns made by you to the Department.

As and when proceeds of collections become available, they will be applied by us in or towards cover of our outstanding acceptances.

You must in any event cover in cash, London funds, at or before their respective maturity dates, all acceptances outstanding hereunder.

Our commission for accepting your drafts will be at the rate of 1% per annum, i.e. $\frac{1}{4}$% on drafts at 90 days or three months sight. In addition, collection commission as already arranged will be payable by you, and all commissions charged by our agents in the importing countries, as well as their and our incidental expenses.

This credit will expire on 16 February 1977, that is, all drafts on us must be drawn and accepted not later than that date.

We enclose our usual form of undertaking,* which please sign and return to us.

Yours faithfully,
WILLIAM CAXTON & CO

DRAWING THE BILLS

When you, The Exporting Company, wish to make use of this credit you draw bills on the accepting house. Let us assume that you have sold goods to The Overseas Importer, Newtown, Atlantis, to the value of £41,850.90, drawing a bill at say 60 days sight direct on them. Under the terms of credit no. S.3217 this would entitle you to draw on William Caxton & Co. a bill for say £36,000.

An example of the bill drawn on William Caxton under this credit appears on the opposite page at fig. 3a. When this bill has been drawn and endorsed, you will send it together with the shipping documents and the bill drawn on The Overseas Importer to William Caxton with a letter as follows:

---

* Forms of agreement and undertaking vary according to the nature of the credit. For an unsecured credit, for example, the form may consist of a very short and simple statement that the borrower agrees to the terms and conditions and undertakes to abide by them and duly put the accepting house in funds when the bills mature. If the credit is a secured one, the form may set out, in addition, the conditions governing the security, and may make clear the lending banker's right to it in the event of default by the borrower.

£36 000-00   LONDON 19th March 1976

21 JUN 1976

At 90 days   after sight pay to the Order
of The Exporting Company ———————

The sum of thirty six thousand pounds Value received.
Drawn under Credit No 5 3217 against shipment of
Agricultural Tractors to Atlantis per SS "Argonaut"

for THE EXPORTING CO.

To   William Caxton & Co.
    London, E.C.2.

DIRECTOR

ACCEPTED
2 MAR 1976
PAYABLE AT
THE CLEARING BANK
ROYAL EXCHANGE, E.C.3
FOR
WILLIAM CAXTON & CO.
DIRECTOR.

for and on behalf of
THE EXPORTING CO.

Director.

FIGURE 3a

An export bill (London acceptance credit) – accepted and endorsed.

THE EXPORTING COMPANY, London EC2

TO MESSRS WILLIAM CAXTON & CO
London EC2   19 March 1976

Dear Sirs,
Revolving acceptance credit no. S.3217
We enclose herewith the full shipping documents covering a shipment of
agricultural tractors to The Overseas Importer, Newtown, Atlantis. We also
enclose our 60-day sight bill, endorsed in blank, drawn on the importers for
£41,850.90. Would you kindly forward these to your agents in Atlantis and
arrange for the presentation of the bill to the importers for acceptance and later
for collection at maturity and remittance of the proceeds to you.

   Under the terms of the above credit we also enclose our 90-day sight bill drawn
on you for £36,000. After acceptance we should be grateful if you would kindly
hand this bill to Gillett Brothers Discount Company Ltd for discount.

   We should be glad if you would debit our account with your acceptance
commission.

   Yours faithfully,
   THE EXPORTING COMPANY

DISCOUNTING THE BILL

You will send a copy of this letter to Gillett Brothers Discount Company Ltd
with a covering note as follows:

THE EXPORTING CO, London EC2

TO GILLETT BROTHERS DISCOUNT COMPANY LTD
65 Cornhill, London EC3V 3PP   19 March 1976

Dear Sirs,
We enclose a copy of a letter which we have to-day sent to Messrs William
Caxton & Co. Will you please pay the proceeds of the discount to the Lombard
Bank, London EC2, for the credit of our account.

   Yours faithfully,
   THE EXPORTING COMPANY

When Gillett Brothers have discounted the bill they will send a discount statement to you. Here is a copy of their statement:

GILLETT BROTHERS DISCOUNT COMPANY LTD,
65 Cornhill, London EC3V 3PP

TO THE EXPORTING COMPANY
London EC2   22 March 1976

We have pleasure in confirming the PURCHASE of the bills listed below. In accordance with instructions the net proceeds have been paid to *The Lombard Bank, EC2, for the credit of your account.*

AMOUNTS	DISCOUNT & PROCEEDS		DUE DATE	NO. OF DAYS
36,000.00	$8\frac{1}{2}\%$	36,000.00 762.90 35,237.10	21 June	91

per pro
GILLETT BROTHERS DISCOUNT COMPANY LTD

THE BILL MATURES

In accordance with the facility letters, you must put the accepting house in funds on or before the due date of the bill. The proceeds of collection of the trade bill drawn on The Overseas Importer will probably have already been received in London by William Caxton and will more than provide the necessary funds. In any event, however, you are responsible for seeing that William Caxton are paid in time to meet the acceptance at its maturity. This completes the transaction, but as the credit is revolving the amount of the bill paid off (in this instance £36,000) automatically becomes available to finance further exports, unless the period of the credit has expired and has not been extended.

II   THE BILL OF EXCHANGE AND THE IMPORTER
(See part two, pp. 39–46)
Here is an example of the procedure when an importer of commodities into this country asks his bank to open a credit in favour of his overseas supplier:

4 – *Irrevocable documentary letter of credit in favour of an overseas exporter opened by a bank or accepting house.*

You, The Importing Co, request your bank or an accepting house, to issue an irrevocable documentary letter of credit in favour of your overseas exporter by filling in a form of application. Here is a specimen of a completed form:

THE IMPORTING CO, Bradford

TO THE LOMBARD BANK LTD
Bradford Yorks   26 March 1976

Dear Sirs,
We should be glad if you would open on our account an irrevocable documentary letter of credit as follows:
1. In favour of The Woolbuying Company, Royal City, Atlantis
2. Advised through the Bank of Atlantis
3. For a sum of £45,000 (forty-five thousand pounds)
4. Valid in Royal City until 28 May 1976 inclusive
5. Available by drafts on you at 90 days sight
6. Against delivery of the following documents:
   (a) Invoice(s)
   (b) Complete set of on board bills of lading to order and endorsed in blank
   (c) Policy of insurance covering amount of invoice plus 10%
7. Evidencing shipment not later than 21 May 1976 of 160 bales of wool
8. For shipment from Atlantis port to UK port
9. Part shipments are not allowed.
We undertake to execute your bank's normal form of indemnity.

Yours faithfully,
THE IMPORTING COMPANY

The manager of the Bradford branch of The Lombard Bank having approved the application will forward it to the foreign department of his bank in London who will issue an irrevocable documentary letter of credit on the lines of the following:

THE LOMBARD BANK, *foreign branch,* London EC3

TO THE WOOLBUYING COMPANY
Royal City, Atlantis   29 March 1976

Dear Sirs,
Credit no. I.C.7929
At the request and for account of The Importing Company, Bradford, we hereby open our irrevocable documentary letter of credit in your favour, subject to the 'Uniform Customs and Practice for Documentary Credits' (1974 Revision) International Chamber of Commerce (Publication No. 290), to the extent of £45,000 (forty-five thousand pounds). This credit is available by your 90 days sight drafts on us which are to be drawn and negotiated in Royal City on or before 28 May 1976, and should be accompanied by:
   Invoice(s)
   Complete set of on board bills of lading to order and endorsed in blank
   Policy of insurance covering amount of invoice plus 10%
evidencing shipment not later than 21 May 1976 from Atlantis port to UK port of 160 bales of wool. Part shipments are not allowed.
   The drafts drawn must bear particulars of the shipment and the clause 'Drawn under credit I.C.7929'.
   We hereby undertake to honour such drafts provided they are drawn and presented in accordance with the terms of this credit.

   Yours faithfully,
   pro Manager   *pro Manager*

   This document will be sent to the Bank of Atlantis, Royal City, Atlantis, with instructions to pass it on to The Woolbuying Company.

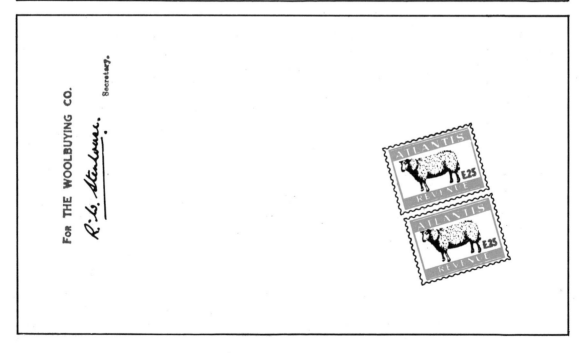

EXCHANGE FOR £44,388 - 39   Royal City, Atlantis 8th April 19 76

At 90 days sight   *pay this* first *Bill of Exchange*
(Second of same tenor and date being unpaid)   *to the Order of*
The Woolbuying Co _____ the sum of
Forty four thousand three hundred and eighty eight pounds
and thirty nine pence. Drawn under Credit I.C. 7929 against shipment
of 160 bales of wool from Atlantis to U.K. per SS " GOLDEN FLEECE".

For and on behalf of
THE WOOLBUYING CO.

To
The Lombard Bank,
Threadneedle Street,
London,
E.C.2.

Director

FOR THE WOOLBUYING CO.

Secretary.

FIGURE 5a
An import bill (irrevocable documentary letter of credit) – accepted and endorsed.

An example of a bill drawn under this credit appears on the opposite page at fig 5a.

The bill when drawn and endorsed by The Woolbuying Company will be handed with the documents to the Bank of Atlantis, or to another local bank. The bank will buy the bill (i.e. will pay the shipper the amount of the bill, less a discount calculated to allow for the time the bill takes to reach London and the period until it matures) from the drawers, and forward it with the documents to their London office or agent. The London office or agent will surrender the documents to the Lombard Bank against acceptance of the bill, and will then either hold the bill until maturity, or discount it by including it in a parcel of bills for sale to a discount house.

THE BILL MATURES

On or before the maturity date of the bill, you, The Importing Company, will have to put the Lombard Bank in funds to meet the bill, or such part of it as you have not already met by making payment to the bank in advance of maturity in order to obtain release of the wool, or of some part of it.

It may be that by special arrangement the bank will have already released to you some or all of the documents of title in advance of payment, whether against a trust receipt or against the deposit by you of other security. In either case the full amount of the face value of the bill must have reached the Lombard Bank on or before the maturity date of the bill.

Here are examples of facility letters which an importer of commodities into the UK might receive from an accepting house:

5 – *Revolving acceptance credit covering shipments of wool to the UK opened in favour of the Importing Company by William Caxton & Co* – unsecured.

WILLIAM CAXTON & CO, London ECA

TO THE IMPORTING COMPANY
Bradford   2 January 1976

Dear Sirs,

Revolving letter of credit no. U.420

With reference to our conversation of yesterday, we have pleasure in opening for your account a revolving acceptance credit to the extent of £750,000 (seven hundred and fifty thousand pounds) running uncovered at any one time, available by your drafts upon ourselves at 3 months sight to finance your purchases of wool in Atlantis and afloat to the United Kingdom.

Drafts are to be enfaced with words indicating the transactions against which they are drawn, e.g. 'drawn under credit no. U.420 against shipments of . . . bales of wool from Atlantis to United Kingdom per s.s. . . .'.

It is understood that the wool underlying acceptances under this credit will be fully insured by you.

All acceptances are to be covered by you in cash with us one day before their respective maturity dates, but, the credit being revolving, fresh drafts up to the amount so covered may then be drawn.

Our acceptance commission, payable at time of acceptance, will be $1\frac{1}{4}\%$ per annum.

This credit expires on 31 December 1976, i.e. bills must be drawn and accepted not later than that date.

We shall be glad if you will kindly sign and return to us the enclosed form of undertaking* in respect of this credit.

We are, dear Sirs,

Yours faithfully,

WILLIAM CAXTON & CO

* See note on p 70

6 – *Revolving acceptance credit covering shipments of wool to the UK opened in favour of the Importing Company by William Caxton & Co* – secured.

WILLIAM CAXTON & CO, London EC2

TO THE IMPORTING COMPANY
Bradford   2 January 1976

Dear Sirs,
Revolving letter of credit no. S.2196
With reference to our conversation of yesterday, we have pleasure in opening for your account a revolving acceptance credit to the extent of £750,000 (seven hundred and fifty thousand pounds) running at any one time, available by your drafts upon ourselves at 3 months sight to finance your purchases of wool to be shipped to the United Kingdom.

Drafts are to be enfaced with words indicating the transactions against which they are drawn, e.g. 'drawn under credit no. S.2196 against shipments of . . . bales of wool from Atlantis to United Kingdom per s.s. . . .'.

When you draw upon us in the first instance, you are to lodge with us, or with our agents in Atlantis, as security, full sets of on board bills of lading,* endorsed to our order or in blank for the raw wool shipped to this country, with the relative invoices.

If desired by you, the bills of lading will be surrendered by us, on arrival of the carrying vessels, to approved storage concerns for storage of the wool in independent warehouses in our name and the relative warrants sent to us.

Your drafts are to be for amounts not exceeding 85% of the invoice value of the wool being shipped and in the event of any decline in the market prices you are on each occasion and forthwith, and without waiting our application, to re-establish and maintain the margin in value by depositing with us either cash or additional wool by way of security.

---

* It will often happen, particularly in the wool trade, that the bills of lading are not yet available either in the UK or in Atlantis, on the day on which you The Importing Company wish to draw your bill. In such a case the credit may provide for you to deposit with the accepting house, William Caxton & Co, some other security, such as, for example, documents of title to other wool of which you are already the owners. In this context see glossary note on 'Red clause', p 100.

It is understood that the wool comprising the security for acceptances under this credit will be fully insured by you and that the relative policies or certificates will be deposited with us.

You may, with our consent, substitute from time to time other wool of not less value for any of the above mentioned security that you may withdraw.

All acceptances are to be covered by you in cash with us one day before their respective maturity dates, but, the credit being revolving, fresh drafts up to the amount so covered may then be drawn subject to the terms and conditions hereof.

In default of reimbursement at maturity of any acceptance or in the event of your failing to maintain the margin of security above stipulated, we are at liberty to sell the whole or any part of the security and apply the proceeds in or towards the liquidation of your indebtedness to us.

Our acceptance commission, payable at time of acceptance, will be $1\frac{1}{4}\%$ per annum.

This credit expires on 31 December, 1976, i.e. bills must be drawn and accepted not later than that date.

We shall be glad if you will kindly sign and return to us the enclosed form of undertaking* in respect of this credit.

We are, dear Sirs,

Yours faithfully,

WILLIAM CAXTON & CO

DRAWING THE BILLS UNDER SECURED CREDIT S.2196

When you wish to make use of the credit you draw bills on the accepting house. Let us assume that you wish to finance a shipment of wool costing £500,000 under the letter of credit S.2196. You will draw bills on William Caxton & Co, for £425,000 (85% of the shipment). It is not customary for bills to be drawn for amounts exceeding £100,000, except by special arrangement, so in fact you would draw five bills, four for £100,000 each and one for £25,000.

An example of a bill drawn under this credit appears on the opposite page at fig 6a.

* See note on p 70

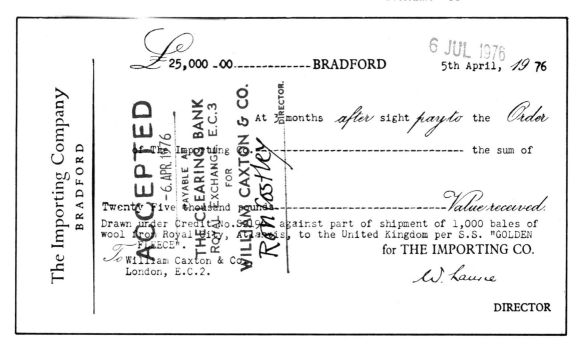

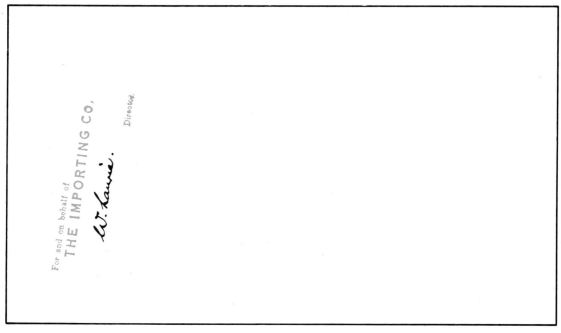

FIGURE 6a

An import bill (London acceptance credit) – accepted and endorsed.

The bills when drawn and endorsed will be sent by you to William Caxton, with a letter of instructions. This might read as follows:

THE IMPORTING COMPANY, Bradford

TO MESSRS WILLIAM CAXTON & CO
London EC2   5 April 1976

Dear Sirs,

Revolving letter of credit no. S.2196

We have been informed by our agents in Atlantis, The Woolbuying Co, Royal City, that they have purchased for our account one thousand bales of wool for a total invoice value of £500,000. In accordance with the above letter of credit we enclose herewith our cheque for £75,000, being 15% of the total price, and five bills totalling £425,000 drawn on you at three months sight.

Please accept these bills and then hand them to Messrs Gillett Brothers Discount Company Ltd, for discount against their cheque for the proceeds. We should be glad if you would then remit to your agents in Royal City, Atlantis the total sum of £500,000 for payment to The Woolbuying Co against the documents of title to the shipment, viz. on board bills of lading, invoice and insurance policy.

If you would kindly notify us of your acceptance commission and the discounting charge we will send you, by return, our cheque in settlement.

Yours faithfully,
THE IMPORTING COMPANY

In the foregoing letter it has been assumed that payment for the wool is to be made by remittance to Atlantis. Alternatively the arrangement made between you and The Woolbuying Co may provide for them to draw a sight bill *on you* which they will negotiate, with the documents of title attached, through their bank, say the Bank of Atlantis, Atlantis. The Bank of Atlantis, having bought the bill, will forward it to their London office who will present it to you. You will pay the bill at sight and receive the documents. You will then reimburse yourself by drawing bills on William Caxton. In this case the letter of instruction might read as follows:

THE IMPORTING COMPANY, Bradford

TO MESSRS WILLIAM CAXTON & CO
London EC2   5 April 1976

Dear Sirs,
Revolving letter of credit no. S.2169
We enclose herewith documents of title covering one thousand bales of wool purchased for a total cost of £500,000 which are now in transit to us from Atlantis per the s.s. *Golden Fleece*. In accordance with the terms of the above credit we also enclose five bills totalling £425,000 drawn on you at three months sight.

We should be grateful if you would accept these bills and then hand them to Messrs Gillett Brothers Discount Company Ltd for discount. If you would kindly notify us of your acceptance commission we will send you by return our cheque in settlement.

Yours faithfully,
THE IMPORTING CO

DISCOUNTING THE BILL

At the same time as you send the bills to the accepting house for acceptance, you will write to the discount house requesting them to discount the bills, and instructing them to whom to pay the proceeds. You will find it useful to make an additional copy of the letter sent to the accepting house, and to send the copy to the discount house, with a covering note.

In the case where the cash is to be remitted to Atlantis, the accepting house is controlling the money and making the payment in Royal City, Atlantis, on your behalf. Therefore the discount house must pay the proceeds of the bills to the accepting house. Here is a specimen of your note to the discount house:

THE IMPORTING COMPANY, Bradford

TO MESSRS GILLETT BROTHERS DISCOUNT COMPANY LTD
65 Cornhill, London EC3V 3PP   5 April 1976

Dear Sirs,
William Caxton & Co—credit no. S.2196
We enclose a copy of a letter which we have to-day written to Messrs William
Caxton & Co, from which you will see that we have asked them to hand to you
five bills totalling £425,000 for discount. We should be glad if you would pay the
proceeds of these bills to William Caxton & Co.

    Yours faithfully,
    THE IMPORTING CO

In the case where you have to meet a sight bill, by drawing a cheque on
your own bank, you would instruct Gillett Brothers to pay the proceeds of the
bills to your bank for the credit of your account.

When the discount house have discounted the bill they will send you a
discount statement. Here is a copy of the statement which you, The Importing Co, would receive in reply to the letter quoted above:

GILLETT BROTHERS DISCOUNT COMPANY LTD
65 Cornhill, London EC3V 3PP

TO THE IMPORTING CO
Bradford, Yorkshire

6 April 1976

We have pleasure in confirming the PURCHASE of the bills listed below. In accordance with instructions the net proceeds have been paid to *William Caxton & Co.*

AMOUNTS	DISCOUNT & PROCEEDS		DUE DATE	NO. OF DAYS
100,000.00				
100,000.00				
100,000.00				
100,000.00		425,000.00	6 July	91
25,000.00	$8\frac{1}{2}$%	9,006.51		
		415,993.49		

per pro
GILLETT BROTHERS DISCOUNT COMPANY LTD

THE BILLS MATURE

In accordance with the terms of the facility, you, the importer must put the accepting house in funds on or before the due date of the bills. You may already have sent William Caxton & Co all or part of the funds due at maturity before the due date, in order to obtain release of the wool, or part of it. Alternatively by lodging documents of title to other wool you can obtain release of the wool shipped, or part of it, without putting the accepting house in funds. In any event the accepting house will have to be paid, on or before maturity, the face value of the bills which they will have to meet on presentation. This completes the transaction, but as the credit is revolving the amount of the bills paid off (in this instance £425,000) automatically becomes available to finance a further shipment unless the period of the credit has expired and has not been extended.

III THE BILL OF EXCHANGE AND THE MANUFACTURER

(See Part two, pp 46–47)

Here is an example of a facility letter which a manufacturer might receive from an accepting house:

7 – *Revolving acceptance credit covering purchases of cocoa, and other materials, opened in favour of* The Manufacturing Co *by* William Caxton & Co – unsecured.

WILLIAM CAXTON & CO, London EC2

TO THE MANUFACTURING CO

Barchester   10 January 1976

Dear Sirs,

Revolving acceptance credit no. U.429

We have pleasure in establishing for you, in response to your application, our revolving acceptance credit no. U.429 to the extent of £300,000 (three hundred thousand pounds) running uncovered by cash at any one time, available by your drafts upon ourselves at usances up to three months date for the purpose of financing your purchases of flour, cocoa beans and other raw materials used in your business.

Such drafts must be enfaced with a brief description of the merchandise against which they are drawn, e.g. 'Drawn against purchase of cocoa beans'.

It is a condition of this credit that the value of the raw materials etc. purchased and in stock, free from lien, must always exceed the total amount of our acceptances outstanding under the credit.*

It is understood that your stocks are kept fully insured against fire and usual risks.

All drafts are to be covered by you in cash with us at or before their respective maturity dates, but, the credit being revolving, when and to the extent that drafts are so covered the facility automatically becomes available again.

Our acceptance commission, payable at time of acceptance, will be $1\frac{1}{4}\%$ per annum.

This credit expires on 31 December 1976, i.e. bills must be drawn and accepted not later than that date.

* William Caxton & Co might require you to give them periodic certificates of your purchases. In some cases they might ask for copies of suppliers' invoices.

We shall be pleased if you will kindly sign and return to us the enclosed form of undertaking,* together with an up-to-date copy of your memorandum and articles of association, copy of a resolution of your board authorising the establishment of the credit, and specimen signatures of those authorised to sign on your behalf in its operation.

We are, dear Sirs,
Yours faithfully,
WILLIAM CAXTON & CO

DRAWING THE BILLS

An example of a bill drawn under this credit appears on the next page at fig 8a.

Your letter sent to William Caxton & Co with the bills might be worded as follows:

THE MANUFACTURING CO, Barchester

TO MESSRS WILLIAM CAXTON & CO
London EC2   1 April 1976

Dear Sirs,
Revolving acceptance credit no. U.429
With reference to the above credit dated 10 January 1976, we should like to avail ourselves of £150,000 of the facility, and enclose herewith five bills, each for £30,000, drawn at three months date, which we have endorsed in blank.

After acceptance kindly hand these bills to Messrs Gillett Brothers Discount Company Ltd for discount.

We should be glad to receive from you in due course your account for the acceptance commission.

Yours faithfully,
THE MANUFACTURING CO

DISCOUNTING THE BILLS

In this case the proceeds of the discount are to be paid to you, the manufacturer, and the discount house must be instructed accordingly.

Here is a specimen letter to the discount house:

* See note on p 70.

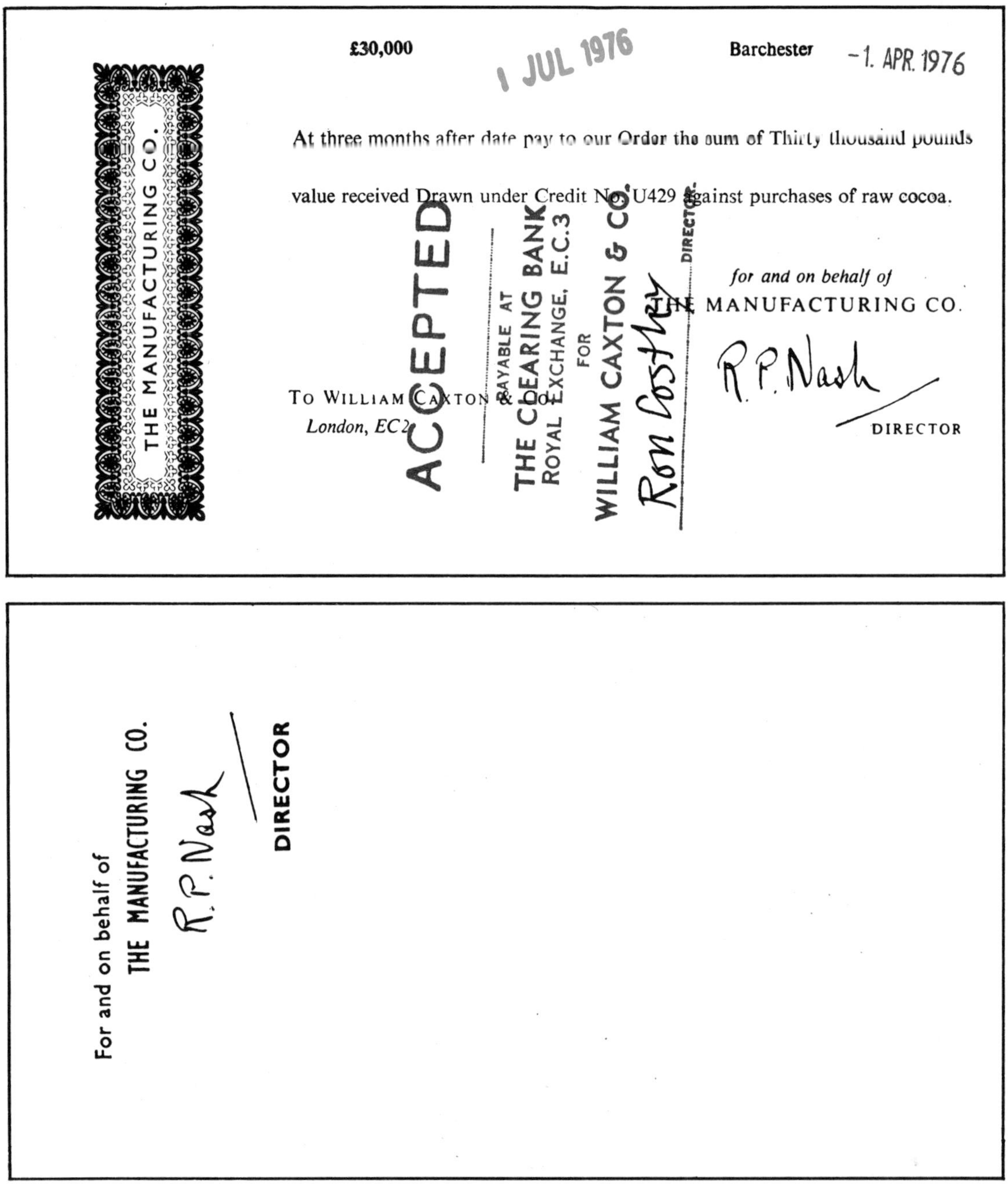

£30,000   1 JUL 1976   Barchester   −1. APR. 1976

At three months after date pay to our Order the sum of Thirty thousand pounds

value received Drawn under Credit No. U429 against purchases of raw cocoa.

THE MANUFACTURING CO.

ACCEPTED

PAYABLE AT
THE CLEARING BANK
ROYAL EXCHANGE, E.C.3
FOR
WILLIAM CAXTON & CO.
Ron Costley
DIRECTOR

To WILLIAM CAXTON & CO.
London, EC2

for and on behalf of
THE MANUFACTURING CO.

R. P. Nash

DIRECTOR

For and on behalf of
THE MANUFACTURING CO.

R. P. Nash

DIRECTOR

FIGURE 8a
A manufacturer's bill – accepted and endorsed.

THE MANUFACTURING CO, Barchester

TO MESSRS GILLETT BROTHERS DISCOUNT COMPANY LTD
65 Cornhill, London EC3V 3PP   1 April 1976

Dear Sirs,

William Caxton & Co—credit no. U.429

We enclose a copy of a letter which we have to-day written to Messrs William
Caxton & Co, from which you will see that we have asked them to hand to you
five bills, totalling £150,000, for discount. We should be glad if you would pay
the proceeds of these bills to The Lombard Bank, London, EC2, for the credit of
our account at their Barchester branch.

Yours faithfully,
THE MANUFACTURING COMPANY

When the discount company have discounted the bill, they will send you
a discount statement. Here is the statement which you would receive:

GILLETT BROTHERS DISCOUNT COMPANY LTD,
65 Cornhill, London EC3V 3PP

TO THE MANUFACTURING COMPANY
Barchester   2 April 1976

We have pleasure in confirming the PURCHASE of the bills listed below. In
accordance with instructions the net proceeds have been paid to *The Lombard
Bank Ltd, EC2, for the credit of your account at their Barchester branch.*

AMOUNTS	DISCOUNT & PROCEEDS		DUE DATE	NO. OF DAYS
30,000.00				
30,000.00				
30,000.00				
30,000.00				
30,000.00		150,000.00	1 July	90
	$8\frac{1}{2}\%$	3,143.84		
		146,856.16		

per pro
GILLETT BROTHERS DISCOUNT COMPANY LTD

THE BILL MATURES

In accordance with the terms of the facility you must put the accepting house in funds on or before the due date of the bill. The credit, being revolving, allows for the drawing of new bills to replace those which are maturing, provided the total value of materials purchased and in stock permits, and you still wish to borrow.

Let us assume that a few days before the 1st July, 1976, when the £150,000 bills drawn on 1st April, 1976, mature, you decide that, owing to an improvement in your liquid position, you can reduce your borrowings under the credit to £90,000.

Here is the sort of letter which you will address to William Caxton & Co:

THE MANUFACTURING CO, Barchester

TO MESSRS WILLIAM CAXTON & CO
London EC2   28 June 1976

Dear Sirs,
Revolving acceptance credit no. U.429
With reference to the five drafts of £30,000 each drawn under the above credit and maturing on 1 July next, we enclose our cheque for £60,000 and three drafts each for £30,000 dated 1 July and drawn at three months after date, which we should be glad if you will kindly accept and hand to Messrs Gillett Brothers Discount Company Ltd for discount on 1 July, against their cheque for the proceeds, which you will apply against the balance of the maturing acceptances.

On receiving from you particulars of your acceptance commission and the discounting charges, we will send you our cheque in settlement by return of post.

Yours faithfully,
THE MANUFACTURING COMPANY

A copy of the above letter will be sent to Gillett Brothers Discount Company Ltd with a covering letter, the wording of which will be similar to that illustrated on page 89 except that Gillett Brothers will be instructed to pay the proceeds to William Caxton & Co.

IV THE BILL OF EXCHANGE AND THE INVESTOR

(See part two, pp 59–60)

I – THE PURCHASE

An investment in bills is most conveniently arranged by teleprinter or by a telephone call, in the course of which there will be agreed:

    the face value of the bills you wish to buy;

    the names of the acceptors;

    their date or dates of maturity;

    the date from which your investment is to run;

    where they are to be delivered;

    the rate of discount;

    the net amount you will be investing.

Gillett Brothers will then send a discount statement to you. Here is a copy of their statement:

GILLETT BROTHERS DISCOUNT COMPANY LTD
65 Cornhill, London EC3V 3PP

TO THE INVESTOR
Birmingham, Warwickshire   15 April 1976

We have pleasure in confirming the SALE to you VALUE 15 April 1976 of the
bills listed below,*

per pro
GILLETT BROTHERS DISCOUNT COMPANY LTD

ACCEPTOR	AMOUNTS	DUE DATE	NO. OF DAYS
The Bank of Atlantis	65,391.40	14 June	60
William Caxton & Co.	36,000.00	21 June	67
The London Blender	29,603.81	25 June	71
William Caxton & Co.	30,000.00	1 July	77
William Caxton & Co.	25,000.00	6 July	82
The Industrial Co.	27,463.04	8 July	84
The Lombard Bank	44,388.39	12 July	88
	257,846.64		
Discount @ 8⅜%	4,361.98		
Net proceeds	253,484.66		

See note on discount rates, page 62

* Here will be inserted:
which we enclose herewith.
in accordance with your instructions they have been handed to The Clearing Bank, Royal
Exchange, EC3
        or
which we have lodged in safe custody. We enclose the safe custody receipt.

2 – DELIVERY

When making your purchase, you will have given instructions where your bills are to be delivered. You may wish them to be:

sent to you by post;

handed to your agent in the City of London;

placed in safe custody under arrangements made by Gillett Brothers.

In each case you will receive the appropriate letter of confirmation (see p 92). If you wish to make use of Gillett Brothers' arrangements for safe custody, no charges will be incurred for the service, and you will receive in due course a letter confirming that it has been done, as follows:

GILLETT BROTHERS DISCOUNT COMPANY LTD
65 Cornhill, London EC3V 3PP

THE INVESTOR
Birmingham, Warwickshire   15 April 1976

Safe Custody Receipt
We have pleasure in informing you that we have to-day placed in safe custody on your behalf with The Clearing Bank, Royal Exchange, London EC3 (Account No. 76).

per pro
GILLETT BROTHERS DISCOUNT COMPANY LTD

ACCEPTORS	DUE DATE TOTALS	DUE DATE	NO. OF DAYS
The Bank of Atlantis	65,391.40	14 June	60
William Caxton & Co.	36,000.00	21 June	67
The London Blender	29,603.81	25 June	71
William Caxton & Co.	30,000.00	1 July	77
William Caxton & Co.	25,000.00	6 July	82
The Industrial Co.	27,463.04	8 July	84
The Lombard Bank	44,388.39	12 July	88
	257,846.64		

It should be mentioned that at the time this edition is being prepared exchange control regulations do not allow sterling bills of exchange to be sent outside the United Kingdom. Bills purchased by a non-resident must be lodged with an authorised depositary.

3 – AT MATURITY

Bills you have bought from Gillett Brothers are payable at a bank. Consequently they need only to be presented at that bank when the due date arrives for them to be paid.

If you are holding the bills yourself, you should hand them to your bank for collection a few days before the maturity date, and your account will be credited with their face value on the due date. If they are in the hands of your London agent, he will do this for you.

If they are deposited under Gillett Brothers' arrangements for safe custody, their face value will be collected at maturity by Gillett Brothers and your instructions sought for the disposal of the funds.

4 – RESALE BEFORE MATURITY

If for any reason you decide to realise your investment in bills before they mature, the procedure in selling them is the same as for the original discounter. A sample of the statement you might receive is on page 73.

Part four
Glossary and index

'When I use a word,
it means just what I choose it to mean
- neither more nor less.'

HUMPTY DUMPTY

ACCEPTING HOUSE: banking house which specialises in accepting bills drawn on it under 'credits' established on behalf of or in favour of approved customers. 13

ACCEPTOR: the person to whom the bill is addressed and who shows his assent by signing his name across the bill, indicating that he will pay the bill at maturity. 15, 25

BANK OF ENGLAND BILLS: bills eligible for discount at the Bank of England are sometimes called 'Bank of England bills'. The bills must bear two good British names, one of which must be the acceptor. The other may be a discount house (by endorsement). Under the terms of Competition and Credit Control, bank acceptances eligible for re-discount at the Bank of England are regarded as Reserve assets. See Reserve assets. 26

BANK RATE: was the advertised rate at which the Bank of England would discount eligible bills of exchange. Bank rate was normally fixed by the directors of the Bank at their weekly meeting each Thursday, but alterations had sometimes been announced upon other days. Now superseded by Minimum Lending Rate. *see* Minimum Lending Rate.

BILLS OF EXCHANGE
– Act, 1882 15, 20
– and the exporter: 31–39 and procedure
– and the continental importer: 55–57
– and the importer; 39–46 and procedure
– and the international trader: 51–57
– and the investor: 59–60 and procedure
– and the manufacturer: 46–47 and procedure
– Bank endorsed: 24, 46
– Bank of England: *see* Bank of England bills
– commercial: bills drawn against a commercial transaction. The expression is also commonly used to cover bills other than Treasury bills and Local Authority bills.
– definition of: 15
– documentary: bills which are supported by various documents, such as bill(s) of lading, invoices, policy of insurance etc. 24
– finance: 26, 49
– fine bank: bills accepted by banks and accepting houses of 'undoubted' standing. 23, 24
– foreign bank: bills accepted by a branch in this country of a bank registered overseas. 23
– foreign domicile: 23, 36, 37
– function of: 20

Bills of exchange, continued]
– interest clause: *see* interest clause bills.
– international: 20
– names thereon: 23
– negotiated: 36, 45, 46
– on LONDON 15, 20, 37, 53
– parties to: 15
– Pig on Pork: bills drawn by one branch of a firm or company on another, or by one person or firm on another intimately connected – the implication being that the bills are not truly two-name bills.
– pre-finance: bills drawn under pre-finance credits *(q.v.)*
– quality of: 22
– re-finance: bills drawn under re-finance credits *(q.v.)*
– remitted: 53–57
– self-liquidating: 25
– sight: 21, 36
– term: 21
– trade: bills drawn by one trader on another against actual trade transactions 23, 24, 35, 45, 49

BILL OF LADING: a receipt for goods upon shipment, signed by the master of the ship or some person authorised to sign it on behalf of the shipowner. On the arrival of the ship at its destination the consignee by handing the bill of lading to the master or local agents of the ship obtains possession of the goods. It is therefore a document of title. A bill of lading is also transferable by endorsement. If a bank is financing the shipment the bills of lading are handed to the bank often attached to and supporting a bill of exchange. 35 and procedure

BUYERS' MARKET: a condition of markets in which goods are plentiful and there is little demand for them so that the buyer makes his own terms.

C.I.F.: Cost, Insurance, Freight. 'Goods imported at £x per ton C.I.F.' means that the price quoted to the buyer includes transit costs and insurance (c.f. F.O.B.)

CLAUSING: the statement on the face of a bill of exchange giving details of the underlying transaction in respect of which the bill is drawn. 25

CLEARING BANK: a member of the London Bankers Clearing House.

COMMISSION
– accepting: a charge made by a bank or

Commission, continued]
accepting house for the use of its name as an
acceptor on bills of exchange.
                 27 and procedure

COST
– of bill finance   27 and procedure

CREDIT
– acceptance: 13, 22, 33, 41 and procedure
– against collections: 35
– back to back: a credit has been opened by a
bank in favour of a trader (frequently a middle
man) covering certain goods. On the strength
and security of the credit another bank opens
a separate credit on behalf of the trader, in
favour of the supplier of the goods. Such an
arrangement may be described as a back to
back credit.
– campaign: credits which were in the past
arranged to provide finance to primary pro-
ducers, in some cases enabling them to pay
their labour and other costs as far back as the
sowing of the crops and the expense incurred
in harvesting, packing and moving the crops
from up country to railhead, and thence to
port, and across the seas to the country to
which they were to be consigned.
– clean: a credit opened by a banker which
provides for bills being drawn upon the
banker without supporting documents being
attached, or without security in any form
being provided.   35, 43
– confirmed: a credit which is opened or issued
by one bank is irrevocable (see below), and in
being notified through another bank (usually
in a different country) is made even stronger
by that other bank adding its own guarantee
that the bills will be paid or accepted if they
are in due order. The bank thus 'confirming' a
credit will charge the opening banker an
additional commission.   33, 67
– definition of   22
– documentary: one method adopted to finance
overseas trade is to insert in a contract for the
sale of goods a provision that payment shall be
made by a banker. The banker, in a letter of
credit, in effect undertakes to pay the price of
the goods, or accept a bill of exchange for the
invoice amount, upon delivery to him of the
invoices and shipping documents. The nature
of the undertaking varies according to whether
the credit is revocable or irrevocable (see
below) or confirmed (see above). Such a
credit is a documentary credit. The banker

Credit, continued]
receives a small percentage commission. Frequently the documents are pledged to the
banker as security.   41, 74
– irrevocable: a letter of credit which, during
the period it is stated to remain in force, cannot be revoked or cancelled by the bankers,
who opened or issued it unless the beneficiary
is agreeable. The bankers undertake to pay or
accept all bills drawn in conformity with its
terms and conditions. (Revocable credits are
sometimes used, but nowadays they are com-
paratively rare).   31, 33, 41, 63, 74
– letter of: 22 and procedure
– opening a: 22
– pre-finance: the term should be 'pre-shipment'
finance. With certain primary commodities
from certain countries (e.g. cotton from Brazil)
it may be expedient to put up the money
before the merchandise is actually shipped,
and bills drawn on London to obtain the
necessary funds are known loosely as pre-
finance bills.
– Red clause: a credit may authorise advances
to the beneficiary to enable payment to be
made for produce before shipment and,
therefore, before bills of lading can be lodged
with the negotiating bank. Advances are
made by the local bank who will negotiate the
drafts, on the beneficiary's statement that they
are required for that purpose. These advances, together with interest, are liquidated
from the proceeds of negotiation of the bill
which is drawn under the credit when the
bill of lading is available. The appellation
'Red clause' is derived from the custom of
printing the clause relating to advances in red
at the foot of the credit. Frequent use of the
Red clause has been made in financing purchases of Australian wool.   79
– re-finance: where an overseas importer of
goods makes an arrangement with London
bankers to effect immediate payment to the
suppliers, and then, when the payment is
made, borrows the money by drawing a time
bill under an acceptance credit which he has
opened for this purpose, and discounts it, this
bill is called a 're-finance' bill. It is a loose
phrase which came into use with exchange
control, and its purpose is largely to distin-
guish that type of bill from the more usual or
traditional case where the suppliers themselves draw the time bills on London at the

Credit, continued]
outset.   57
– revolving: a 'revolving' credit in its simplest and generally understood form, is a credit of which it is a condition that any portion used by the borrower and reimbursed to the banker during the period of validity of the credit becomes available again, within the terms and conditions of the credit, *automatically upon* such reimbursement. The credit thus permits an indefinite amount in total, but has a stated limit to the amount of drafts that may be outstanding at any one time.   33
– transferable: a credit where the paying, accepting or negotiating bank is authorised to transfer all or part of the credit to a new beneficiary at the request of the original beneficiary. Such credits are used for various reasons, but they are of particular help to original beneficiaries who are agents or middle men, to whom they are a convenient way of paying the actual supplier of the goods without having themselves to arrange a credit or find temporary finance.
– unconfirmed: 67
DEPOSIT RATE: the rate of interest which banks allow on deposits.
DISCOUNT: the amount of deduction calculated at an agreed rate, per cent per annum, which is allowed for immediate payment of the amount of a term bill, which has still a period to run before its maturity.   27, 28
DISCOUNTING: 19–20, 26, and procedure
DISCOUNT MARKET: is not a particular place or building but consists of eleven discount companies who make a market by dealing in money, bills of exchange, British government Treasury bills and short-dated bonds, Local Authority bills and bonds, sterling certificates of deposit, dollar certificates of deposit and also bills of exchange in currencies other than sterling.
DOCUMENTS: 74
DOCUMENTS AGAINST ACCEPTANCE (d/a): a banker may receive instructions from the correspondent sending the bill to deliver up the documents to the drawee upon the latter accepting the bill.   45
DOCUMENTS AGAINST PAYMENT (d/p): a banker may have instructions to give up the documents on payment of a demand or sight bill, or of a term bill under rebate *(q.v.)*   35
DRAWEE: the person to whom the bill is

Drawee, continued]
addressed i.e. drawn upon. When he has signed on the bill an undertaking to pay it he is called the acceptor.   15
DRAWER: The person who signs a bill of exchange giving an order to another person, the drawee, to pay the amount mentioned therein. By drawing the bill he engages that on presentation it shall be accepted and paid according to its tenor, and if it be dishonoured he will compensate the holder or any endorser who is compelled to pay it provided that the requisite proceedings on dishonour be fully taken. A bill may be drawn payable to or to the order of, the drawer, the drawee, or some other payee, or to bearer.   15, 25
EASTERN EXCHANGE BANK: a bank, with branches mainly in eastern countries, engaged in financing trade between those countries and other parts of the world, and dealing in foreign exchange.
ENDORSEE: the person to whom a bill or cheque is assigned by way of endorsement. If and when endorsement is made without assignment the bill is said to be 'endorsed in blank'.
ENDORSER: when the payee signs his name on the back of a bill or cheque he is called the 'endorser' and when the instrument is negotiated to other persons each person may endorse it in turn and become an endorser. Each endorser of a bill is liable thereon.   15
EXPORT CREDITS GUARANTEE DEPT: 36 and Procedure
FINE RATE: the lowest to the seller of fine bank bills, i.e. the most favourable rate of discount.
F.O.B.: Free on board. 'Goods imported at £x per ton F.O.B.' means that the price quoted to the buyer only includes putting them on board ship; all freights and insurances must be paid by the buyer.
HOLDER: the person who is in possession of a bill, who may be either the payee, an endorser, or the bearer.
HYPOTHECATION: for our purposes, this may be simply defined as making over or assigning to lenders, as security, goods or documents of title thereto, by written agreement creating a pledge on the goods.   35, 43
INDORSER: *see* Endorser
INTEREST CLAUSE BILL: a bill may be drawn for a fixed amount plus interest at a stated rate per annum from the time of negotiation

Interest clause bill, continued]

or date of the bill until proceeds of the bill are received. Such bills are usually met in the eastern and Australian trade and are not seen in the London discount market.

MATURITY: the date upon which a bill matures or falls due to be paid. A bill which matures on a Sunday, or a bank holiday, becomes payable on the succeeding business day.

MINIMUM LENDING RATE: Previously known as Bank rate. The minimum rate at which the Bank, acting as lender of last resort, normally lends to members of the discount market against security of Treasury bills, other approved bills, or government stocks with five years or less to maturity. From 13 October 1972, the rate is automatically set $\frac{1}{2}\%$ higher than the average rate of discount for Treasury bills established at the weekly tender, rounded to the nearest $\frac{1}{4}\%$ above. The rate becomes effective, for lending by the Bank, from the following Monday. Special changes in the rate are not excluded under this system, in which event the operation of the formula is temporarily suspended until market rates have adjusted themselves to the new rate.

NEGOTIABLE INSTRUMENT: 13

PAYEE: the person named on a bill to whom or to whose order, payment is directed to be made. Where a bill is not payable to bearer the payee must be named or otherwise indicated therein with reasonable certainly.   15

PRESENTATION FOR ACCEPTANCE: when a bill of exchange is presented to a drawee in order that it may be accepted by him, it is 'presented for acceptance'.

PROCEDURE: 61 *et seq*

REBATE: an allowance, calculated at a rate of interest agreed for the purpose, made to the acceptor of a bill or to the person for whose account a bill has been accepted, when he puts up the money to meet the bill before its maturity date.   45

RED CLAUSE: *see* credit – Red clause

REDISCOUNT: when the discounter of a bill sells it, he is said to 'rediscount' the bill.

RESERVE ASSETS: comprise balances with the Bank of England (other than special and supplementary deposits); money at call (secured and immediately callable) with the listed discount market institutions (discount houses, discount brokers and the money trading departments of listed banks) and with

Reserve assets, continued]

listed brokers (money brokers and jobbers on the stock exchange); British government and Northern Ireland government Treasury bills; UK local authority bills eligible for rediscount at the Bank of England; commercial bills eligible for rediscount at the Bank of England – up to a maximum of 2% of eligible liabilities; British government stocks and stocks of nationalised industries guaranteed by the Government with one year or less to final maturity. The reserve ratio is the total of reserve assets as a percentage of the total of eligible liabilities. Each bank is required to maintain reserve assets amounting to at least $12\frac{1}{2}\%$ of its eligible liabilities.

SECURITY: when a bank or accepting house opens a documentary credit the documents may be pledged as security. A marginal cash deposit is often required to cover any depreciation which may occur in the price of the relative goods.   35, 43

SELLERS' MARKET: a condition of markets in which goods are scarce and there is great demand for them so that the seller makes his own terms.   21

SHIPPING DOCUMENTS: 74 and Procedure

SIGHT: bills may be payable at sight or 'on demand', i.e. immediately on presentation to the drawees. The expression 'after sight' on a term bill of exchange means, literally, after the drawee has seen it. But presentation for 'sighting' cannot be a mere private exhibition to the drawee, the 'sighting' must appear on the bill, in a legal way.   21

SUM PAYABLE: the sum payable by a bill is a sum certain within the meaning of the Bills of Exchange Act even if it is required to be paid:

(*a*) with interest

(*b*) according to an indicated rate of exchange or according to a rate of exchange to be ascertained as directed by the bill.

TENOR: the period of time, as stated or indicated on the bill, for which a bill is drawn to run before it matures. For example 'At sight'; or 'At 90 days after sight'; or 'Three months after date'; or 'On 30th June, 1976'.

TRUST RECEIPT: when documents of title to merchandise which have been pledged to bankers as security for credit facilities are released by the bankers to the borrower in trust,

Trust receipt, continued]
without payment, or without substitution of other security, for some specific purpose, for example to enable him to sell the merchandise, or prepare it for sale or warehouse it, the bankers may ask him to sign a form of receipt embodying the conditions of release, and called a trust receipt.   41, 77

USANCE: strictly speaking this means the time allowed by custom for the currency of bills of exchange in trade between two particular countries. To-day, the word is also frequently used to mean the period of time for which any bill is drawn.   21, 36

VALUE:
– holder for: a person who holds a bill for which value has at some time been given though not necessarily by the holder himself.

WITHOUT RECOURSE: the drawer of a bill, or any endorser, may insert thereon an express stipulation:
   (a) Negativing or limiting his own liability to the holder.
   (b) Waiving as regards himself some or all of the holder's duties.

Bills are sometimes drawn without recourse but bills so marked become one-name bills and are not so well regarded on the discount market as two-name bills.